D0516022

Hallmark
Keepsake Ornaments

The Inside Stories From the Artists Who Create Them

John Peterson

Keepsake Christmas Ornaments
The Inside Stories From the Artists Who Create Them

Copyright © 2007 Hallmark Licensing, Inc.

Published by Hallmark Books,
a division of Hallmark Cards, Inc.,
Kansas City, MO 64141
Visit us on the web at www.Hallmark.com.

All rights reserved. No part of this publication may be reproduced,
transmitted, or stored in any form or by any means
without the prior written permission of the publisher.

Editor: Jeff Morgan
Art Director: Kevin Swanson
Designer: Sarah Smitka/The Pink Pear Design Co.
Production Artist: Dan Horton

ISBN: 978-1-59530-163-5

BOK6072

Printed and bound in China

First Edition, June 2007

10 9 8 7 6 5 4 3 2 1

—

On the front cover, from left to right:
Robot Parade 1, 2000, 1695QX6771, Nello Williams
Santas From Around the World: USA, 2004, 1295QP1731, Edythe Kegrize
Rockin' With Santa, 2005, 2800QLX7622, Sharon Visker
Nostalgic Houses and Shops 23: Corner Bank, 2006, 1500QX2576, Don Palmiter
The Beauty of Birds 1: Northern Cardinal, 2005, 1495QX2135, Edythe Kegrize
On the front flap: The Workshop Clock, 2006, 2600QXC6006, Robert Chad
On the title page: Santas From Around the World: England, 2005, 1295QXG4822, Edythe Kegrize
On page 144: MegaRocketron 3000, 2006, 1650QLX7583
On the back cover: Fairy Messenger 1: Poinsettia Fairy, 2005, 995QX2145, Kristina Kline

Hallmark
Keepsake Ornaments

The Inside Stories From the Artists Who Create Them

GIFT BOOKS
from Hallmark

1500QX3326

Contents

Welcome 6

—

Foreword 8

—

Keepsake Ornament History 10

—

Artist Linda Sickman Looks Back 16

—

Inside Stories From Keepsake Artists 20

—

A Magic Ornament Takes Shape 116

—

Artist Profiles 120

—

The Keepsake Ornament Club 132

—

Index of Ornaments 140

(OPPOSITE) YULETIDE TREASURES 1: SANTA, 2006, EDYTHE KEGRIZE

Welcome

From the earliest days of our company, Hallmark has helped people foster and celebrate relationships, both old and new. The importance of relationships is never more evident to me than at Christmastime. Not only is this a time when friends get in touch and families come together, but it's also a time to blend the past with the present.

Each year, when my wife Jill and I decorate our Christmas tree, we display ornaments from our parents' collections next to newer ornaments we have purchased with our children. Year after year, our Christmas ornaments help celebrate important family events while stirring treasured memories of past holidays.

Even though my daughter is now in college, I still vividly remember the Christmas when she was just five years old. That Christmas morning, she exhibited the typical excitement of a child who has just been visited by Santa. She was especially eager to give me a gift she had picked out for me.

She said, "Daddy, this is something you are really going to like!"

I unwrapped the small package to find a Keepsake ornament. It was Golf's a Ball, which features a snowman made from three golf balls.

As soon as I opened it, my daughter said: "See, Daddy! It's a snowman, and you love to make snowmen. And it's made out of golf balls, and you love to play golf! See, Daddy! Don't you love it?"

I do love that ornament, and I will always remember the excitement and joy on my little girl's face when she gave it to me.

Memories of joy, traditions, and relationships...this is why Hallmark takes such pride in creating Christmas ornaments. It's, undoubtedly, the same reason people enjoy collecting them.

My grandfather, Hallmark founder J.C. Hall, certainly understood this. My dad, Don Hall, understood this, too. It was under their leadership in 1973 that Hallmark began creating Christmas ornaments, and I'm grateful and proud to carry on that legacy.

Some might say we are a greeting card company that makes Christmas ornaments. But making ornaments has been a natural progression of what we do. Keepsake ornaments are more than decorations. Like greeting cards, they speak to what's universal in the human heart by helping people preserve memories, commemorate milestones, and nurture relationships.

That emotional component also must be what so closely ties the people who collect Keepsake ornaments to the Hallmark artists who create them. At signing events across the country each year, Keepsake ornament collectors have the opportunity to meet and talk to the artists. It's clear to me that getting to know the artists makes the ornaments even more valuable to those who purchase and enjoy them.

I hope this book will serve the same purpose, that the artists' personal stories will give readers insights into the relationships that influence the ornaments' creation. The stories are not unique. They reflect the artists' experiences as parents, sisters, brothers, and friends–everyday relationships many of us share. When combined, however, with a gift for creative expression, these experiences come to life, making each ornament a timeless carrier of connection.

I hope you enjoy the pages that follow. May the words and pictures bring added meaning to your own treasured holiday moments–both of Christmases past and of those yet to come.

Don Hall Jr.

DON HALL, JR., CEO OF HALLMARK CARDS, INC. WAS GENERAL MANAGER OF KEEPSAKE, 1993-1995.

Editor's Foreword

In 1972, Hallmark Cards, Inc. sent the same four Christmas ornaments to selected retailers in the United States. They were ball ornaments, the format with which everyone of that time was familiar. What was new and different about them was the Hallmark-designed artwork printed on a transparent band encircling each ornament: four ornaments, four original designs. Hallmark wanted each retailer to look at them and answer a question that was, essentially, "Do you think you could sell something like this in your store?"

In 1973, the product line was launched with 18 ornaments. No one, not even the most wildly optimistic of product planners, knew or imagined that 34 years later, Hallmark's Keepsake Ornament line for Christmas 2007 would include almost 300 ornaments. No one knew or imagined then that Hallmark Christmas ornaments would become so popular that they would eventually support a club with chapters throughout the United States and Canada. The Keepsake Ornament Club, which was nationally organized in 1987 and celebrates its twentieth anniversary in the year of this book's publication, grew from many local clubs formed without sponsorship by people who love the ornaments.

While Keepsake Ornaments have long been available for other holidays and everyday occasions, this book pays tribute to the entrepreneurial spirit of 1972-1973 by focusing on Keepsake Christmas Ornaments. It is largely a collection of stories about how those ornaments come into being–stories told, through Hallmark writer John Peterson, by the people who create the ornaments.

Jeff Morgan
Kansas City, Missouri
January 2007

2400QLX7596

Keepsake Time Line

1972
Hallmark mails boxes, each containing four ball ornaments decorated with original artwork, to drugstores in order to test marketability of an ornament line.
250XHD1035
ELVES

1974
The art of Norman Rockwell and Currier & Ives appears on Keepsake Ornaments.
250QX1061
NORMAN ROCKWELL

1973
First ornament line, made up of 18 ball ornaments, ships—including a dated Betsey Clark First Edition design. The new line will later become Keepsake Ornaments.
250XHD1102
BETSEY CLARK, FIRST IN SERIES

1975
First handcrafted ornaments are offered as well as first licensed properties, including Marty Links™ and Raggedy Ann®
350QX1291
NOSTALGIA: SANTA AND SLEIGH

1976
"Twirl-Abouts" (movable ornaments) debut and Baby's First Christmas is the industry's first commemorative ornament.
450QX1721
TWIRL-ABOUT SANTA

1977
Mickey Mouse and Disney characters as well as the PEANUTS Gang are introduced. Delayed production results in limited quantities of the Betsey Clark ornament.
350QX2642
BETSEY CLARK 5: TRUEST JOYS OF CHRISTMAS

1978

The art of Joan Walsh Anglund joins the line. Chrome-plated chimes and the "25th Christmas Together" ornament make their first appearances.

350QX2696

25TH CHRISTMAS TOGETHER

1979

Here Comes Santa series makes its debut. Other firsts include an ornament for teachers and a handcrafted Baby's First Christmas design.

900QX1559

HERE COMES SANTA 1: SANTA'S MOTOR CAR

1980

First pressed-tin ornament makes its appearance. And the popular, long-running Frosty Friends series is introduced.

550QX1381

SANTA'S FLIGHT

1981

First in the Rocking Horse series gallops in. Photo holder ornaments and plush stuffed animal ornaments debut.

900QX4222

ROCKING HORSE 1

1982

Tin Locomotive series makes its debut, as do ornaments based on hand-embroidered fabric, sculptured acrylic, and cloisonné.

1300QX4603

TIN LOCOMOTIVE 1

1983

The first complete guide to Hallmark Keepsake Ornaments is published. Commemorative ornaments are introduced in a new ceramic bell format.

650QX4307

TENTH CHRISTMAS TOGETHER

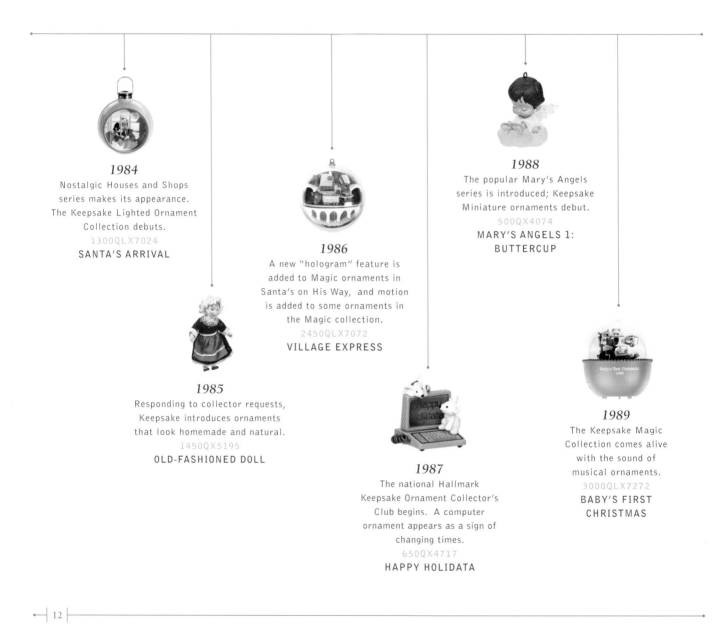

1984

Nostalgic Houses and Shops
series makes its appearance.
The Keepsake Lighted Ornament
Collection debuts.
1300QLX7024
SANTA'S ARRIVAL

1985

Responding to collector requests,
Keepsake introduces ornaments
that look homemade and natural.
1450QX5195
OLD-FASHIONED DOLL

1986

A new "hologram" feature is
added to Magic ornaments in
Santa's on His Way, and motion
is added to some ornaments in
the Magic collection.
2450QLX7072
VILLAGE EXPRESS

1987

The national Hallmark
Keepsake Ornament Collector's
Club begins. A computer
ornament appears as a sign of
changing times.
650QX4717
HAPPY HOLIDATA

1988

The popular Mary's Angels
series is introduced; Keepsake
Miniature ornaments debut.
500QX4074
**MARY'S ANGELS 1:
BUTTERCUP**

1989

The Keepsake Magic
Collection comes alive
with the sound of
musical ornaments.
3000QLX7272
**BABY'S FIRST
CHRISTMAS**

1990

The national club officially begins to support local clubs, which have been flourishing at the grassroots level for more than a decade. Mom-to-Be and Dad-to-Be commemorative ornaments first appear.

575QX4916

MOM-TO-BE

1992

Cheerful Santa is the first African-American figural Santa ornament. Santa greets callers on Santa's Answering Machine, and Mr. Spock makes a greeting from the Shuttlecraft Galileo™.

975QX5154

CHEERFUL SANTA

1994

Ornaments based on sports figures are introduced and The Beatles Gift Set marks the 30th anniversary of the Fab Four's debut. A Magic Ornament called The Eagle Has Landed commemorates the 25th anniversary of the first lunar landing.

2400QLX7486

THE EAGLE HAS LANDED

1991

The first *STAR TREK*™ ornament and the Classic American Cars series are introduced. The first Hallmark Keepsake Ornament Collector's Club convention is held in Kansas City.

2000QLX7199

STARSHIP ENTERPRISE™

1993

The Holiday BARBIE™ series, personalized Keepsake Ornaments, and a recordable Magic Ornament all debut.

3500QLX7476

MESSAGES OF CHRISTMAS

1995

Two Joe Montana ornaments are offered—in both San Francisco 49ers' and Kansas City Chiefs' uniforms. The art of Marjolein Bastin appears in the Showcase Collection.

1895QK1077

NATURE'S SKETCHBOOK: CHRISTMAS CARDINAL

1996

Keepsake launches an eight-city artist signing event called Artists on Tour. The LIONEL Train® and Madame Alexander™ series attract new collectors.

1895QX5531

LIONEL® TRAINS 1: 700E HUDSON STEAM LOCOMOTIVE

1998

Keepsake Ornaments hosts a big 25th anniversary celebration in Kansas City, Missouri. Keepsake offers Joyful Messenger as a 25th Anniversary Special Issue ornament.

1895QXI6733

JOYFUL MESSENGER (25TH ANNIVERSARY SPECIAL ISSUE)

2000

The Robot Parade series is introduced, and the beginning of a new millennium is the perfect time for the debut of the Cool Decade series.

1495QX6771

ROBOT PARADE 1

1997

NFL and NBA collections and the introduction of The Sky's the Limit series boost Keepsake's appeal for men.

1495QX5574

SKY'S THE LIMIT 1: THE FLIGHT AT KITTY HAWK

1999

Laser Creations brings a new technology—and a new type of ornament—to Keepsake Ornaments.

695QLZ4249

LASER CREATIONS: WISH FOR PEACE

2001

Five lovely sprites join the Keepsake line in the Frostlight Faeries design collection.

3500QP1662

FROSTLIGHT FAERIES: QUEEN AURORA

2002

Santa's Big Night is
the Collector's Club
exclusive ornament.

GiftQXC2002

SANTA'S BIG NIGHT

2004

The Town and Country series
comes to an end, and the Father
Christmas series begins.

1695QX8201

TOWN AND COUNTRY 6:
HOMETOWN CHURCH

2003

Keepsake celebrates its
30th anniversary and the
20th anniversary of
Nostalgic Houses and Shops.

1995QX2467

NOSTALGIC HOUSES AND SHOPS:
TOWN HALL AND MAYOR'S
CHRISTMAS TREE
(SPECIAL ANNIVERSARY EDITION)

2006

The tradition of blending art,
innovation, and leading-edge
technology continues in the
Keepsake line.

4200QLX7616

ROCK CANDY RAILROAD

2005

With sound and light, Maxine
magically sings her crabby versions
of popular Christmas carols.

1995QLX7592

THE CRABBY CAROLER

Linda Sickman
Knows Keepsake History

Linda Sickman's career as a Hallmark artist began in 1963, and she was among the four artists who made up Hallmark's first ornament-sculpting studio. From the start, her creative innovations added significantly to the success of the Keepsake Ornament line. In this interview, which was conducted on Jan. 11, 2007, she was asked to look back over her years at Keepsake Ornaments and reflect on the changes she's seen.

What would you say is the main difference in how ornaments are planned and created now, compared with 30 years ago?

LINDA—When Keepsake Ornaments first started, there were only four artists. Getting a design approved was so simple in those days. The art director would come to each of our booths, look at a design, and say, "It looks good to me, what do you think?" We had answers right then and there, compared to now, when we have to show the design to so many people in committee after committee.

Of course, in the beginning, we didn't have 300 ornaments in the line. It was a much smaller line and it was easier to manage. We'd turn in sketches, and the art director would say, "We don't want too many Santa Clauses, or angels, or whatever." The artists had more input as to what the line was going to look like. But as I said, it was a smaller line. Things were much more simple back then.

There's also been a big change over the years in the materials we make ornaments from. When we first started out, styrene was the only thing we knew about. Now, in addition to styrene, we do blown glass, porcelain, cast metal, tin, cloth—a whole gamut of materials.

And in the beginning, we just had industrial clay to sculpt with. Now we have wood, wax, fabrics, and we can get a lot of different textures. Our quality has improved tremendously—not only in manufacturing, but in artistic ability, too.

Also, we do a lot of market testing now that we didn't do in the early days.

So this means we do finished work that never makes it to the market because it doesn't test well or doesn't meet the parameters of the marketing strategy.

Are there one or two particular factors that helped take the early ornament line to what it is today?

LINDA—When the (Keepsake Ornament) Club was started, it just advanced us a tremendous amount. At the very beginning, who knew ornaments would turn into such a popular product? We couldn't imagine collecting would take off the way it did, so we didn't think in terms of series.

For instance, the Rocking Horse series I did didn't start off as a series. I made one rocking horse, and I painted it. Then I asked for another prototype and another and another, and I painted them all and ended up with a variety of them. Because you can't just paint one and say that's it. (Laughs.) So I painted this group of rocking horses, and I took them into committee and said, "I can't make up my mind. I think they're all great." Fortunately, they liked them all, too, and they said, "Maybe we can make them into a series." So the intent to have a series wasn't there at the beginning, but after seeing the variety of things you could do with a good idea, we got the idea for a series.

Besides the popularity of ornament collecting, what's another big surprise you've seen over the years?

LINDA—That would be probably in manufacturing. Sometimes you can create something, but the big question is whether it can be manufactured. Our manufacturing companies have done a phenomenal job duplicating what we've sculpted. And here at Hallmark—our molding department is terrific at being able to make molds for what we sculpt.

Over the years, all the artists have had to learn what the parameters are for what we can sculpt and what we need to stay away from. We might be able to sculpt a really nice piece, but then it gets changed in manufacturing because of the limitations of material or design. So you learn that if you make something out of ceramics, you need to upsize the original because ceramics shrink. If you make something that's going to be cold cast, you have to consider weight, because it's solid. If it's styrene, it's hollow, but you can't get the texture. The artist needs to know the material—and that was something we all had to learn.

Has your relationship with collectors and other Keepsake devotees influenced your work?

LINDA—All the artists have learned a lot from collectors. In meeting people at signings, we get a lot of suggestions. Sometimes they're ideas we've already had or are getting ready

1300QX4603

1500QLX7083

900QX4222

to do. With Tin Locomotives or the other train series I've done, people would always suggest doing this or that train from a certain year. But my trains are never actual trains that really existed. They're all made up. I might look up the trains people have mentioned and use them as research.

Also, I like to find out what people's hobbies are, what their children or their grandchildren are doing. I get ideas from the things people are interested in.

Imagine you could only keep one of the many ornaments you've created. What would it be?

LINDA—(Laughs) It isn't that every ornament I've done is a precious piece, but I would have a hard time picking out just one. There is one ornament, though, that I've always said is my favorite. It's called Gentle Blessings. It's a peek-through ball with a scene inside of the Baby Jesus and the animals, and you can put a light in through the top. And that represents to me what Christmas is all about. That ornament is from a long time ago, but it still means Christmas to me.

I also love a lot of my tin ornaments. Tin ornaments are lightweight, you can get a variety of colors on them, and they're nostalgic. It's just fun to create tin ornaments because of the process you go through to get it.

What are some of your best memories over the years?

LINDA—My best memories are the times when we laughed. There was an artist named Ed Seale who sat next to me years ago. Ed had worked on this little baby crib ornament for a week. And one day he dropped it on the floor, and when he bent down to pick it up, his chair rolled over it. And that was the end of that design. He had to start all over on it. So it's funny things that have happened to all of us that are my best memories.

During your time as a Keepsake artist, what is one important thing you've learned about the creative process?

LINDA—That it's run amok? (Laughs.) Occasionally, artists are given time to go to the creative workshop that Hallmark has. There we can spend some time blue-skying and renewing our creative juices. It might take a few days to get away from the structure that we're used to—to be able to open your mind up and say, "What else can I do?" The idea is just to explore ideas. That's a phase of the creative process that sometimes gets neglected, but it's so important. You need to let the cows graze. ❀

(TOP, CLOCKWISE) TIN LOCOMOTIVE 1, 1982; ROCKING HORSE 1, 1981; GENTLE BLESSINGS, 1986

The Inside Stories

The Inspiration and Artistry Behind Keepsake Ornaments

ST. NICK, 2006, NINA AUBE

1000PR3945

The First Four

Sue Tague's Elves Were There at the Start

Artist Sue Tague can personally trace Keepsake Ornaments' history back full circle–and for her the circle is actually a ball ornament.

The story really begins with four ball ornaments decorated with original artwork–something that hadn't been seen on the market before.

On December 13, 1972, Hallmark explored the ornament marketing potential by shipping boxes, each containing four ball ornaments, to drug stores around the country. An accompanying letter asked the drug store owners to evaluate the ornament samples–because they might be part of a new Hallmark product line.

One of the ornaments in the box was called Elves, and Sue's original artwork was on it. The others were Betsey Clark (Musicians), Santa With Elves, and Manger Scene.

Needless to say, those who saw the ornaments were enthusiastic. The original four ornaments went from being samples for drug store owners to becoming part of the first Keepsake Ornaments line–comprised of only 18 ornaments–shipped in 1973.

After her initial ornament success, it took Sue almost 20 years to officially become a Keepsake Ornaments artist. Though she began working for Hallmark in 1964, she joined the Keepsake studio in 1994. For most of her Hallmark career she illustrated greeting cards and books–specializing in a kind of character style called "charmers." In fact, it was her illustrations of charming little elves that earned her the chance to join the select group of artists designing the first set of Hallmark ornaments.

"I had done drawings of tiny elves in Little Seeds of Wisdom, which was a card line that was made into a gift book," Sue recalls. "Since elves are part of holiday legend, I was asked to design an ornament with elves." And the rest is history. Sue says she's still a bit surprised at how quickly Keepsake Ornaments became popular.

"At the time, I hadn't seen Christmas ornaments with original artwork on them," she recalls. "I remember asking myself if anyone would like them. I guess they did!" ❋

(TOP LEFT, CLOCKWISE) **ELVES, 1973; MANGER SCENE, 1973; BETSEY CLARK (MUSICIANS), 1973; SANTA WITH ELVES, 1973**

250XHD1035

250XHD1022

250XHD1015

250XHD1002

1275QX4319

1495QX8073

1495QX8129

Classic Cars

For the Guys...Hot American Wheels

I t took a small group of guys staging a polite revolution, led by artist Don Palmiter, to get the Classic American Cars series rolling in 1991.

Now, in hindsight, it makes sense that ornaments for men would sell well. Most Keepsake customers may be women, but they buy for the men in their lives. And men collect stuff pertaining to their interests—cars, trucks, sports—so why not car ornaments?

But back in 1990, Don's car ornament sketches had been rejected three years running. "Up until then, the line was all cute little characters and critters," Don remembers. "There was nothing specifically for guys."

So Don gathered the troops. Keepsake's technical art manager at the time was a car collector who owned a classic 1957 Corvette®. The Keepsake sculpting studio boss was a classic car restorer. The art director had worked on a classic car calendar for Hallmark—and it had sold like gangbusters. Instead of sketches this time, Don submitted a sculpted model of the '57 Corvette. And the other guys lent their vocal support to the proposal.

"This time we all talked our marketing folks into a car series," Don smiles.

Keepsake features an array of ornaments for guys now. And Don—known as the Keepsake "Wheel Guy"—still loves sculpting his Classic American Cars. For him, it's personal.

"I'm heavily into wheels," he says. "I've owned collector cars all along—everything from a 1962 Corvair™ convertible to a Rolls-Royce Silver Cloud III. I've always had at least one really neat car around."

The series lets him study all the details that made each year's model so special. That means going to car shows and taking lots and lots of pictures from every angle. Then there's the paint colors that have gone in and out of fashion over the years. "I try to pick a color that was extremely popular at the time," he says. There's the pink 1959 Series 62 Cadillac®, for instance, and the turquoise 1957 Chevrolet®.

Since that first Corvette in 1991, Don has sculpted four Corvette ornaments for the series, including the 1963 Corvette Sting Ray™ Coupe (2003)–the "split window" coupe, the most sought-after Corvette for collectors. Don explains why there are so many Corvette ornaments in the line. "It's the first and only continuing American sports car," he says. "Collectors love them." He should know—he owns a 2002 Corvette himself.

Classic muscle cars have also grown in popularity in recent years, so Don makes sure they're represented in the series. A favorite ornament of his is the 1970 Ford Mach 1 Mustang (2002). It's a car that really tore up the highway in its day. And it looks pretty cool on a Christmas tree, too.❄

(TOP LEFT, CLOCKWISE) CLASSIC AMERICAN CARS 1: 1957 CORVETTE, 1991; CLASSIC AMERICAN CARS 12: 1970 FORD MACH 1 MUSTANG, 2002; CLASSIC AMERICAN CARS 13: 1963 CORVETTE STING RAY COUPE, 2003

Frosty Friends

Good Ideas Keep Series Going Strong

E d Seale thinks he knows what makes a successful ornament series. "It's the potential for generating ideas without exhausting the possibilities too early," he says.

Ed is the sculptor most associated with Frosty Friends, one of Keepsake Ornaments' longest-running series. It began in 1980, about the time Keepsake's dedicated art studio was being formed, and Ed joined its small, exclusive group of sculptors. Ed sculpted his first Frosty Friends ornament in 1982 and created all but a few of the series' ornaments until his retirement in 2003. In almost 25 years of sculpting ornaments, Ed says Frosty Friends is the series that collectors ask him about most often.

The characters in Frosty Friends usually include an Eskimo child (whether boy or girl has always been open for debate), a penguin, a husky pup, and a polar bear cub. No matter that penguins and polar bears live on different ends of the earth. As Ed says, "All the scenes are a blend of fantasy and reality. We take a lot of artistic license with it."

The ornaments' artistic style is simple and whimsical. And the theme is always the same–the warmth of fun and friendship in an icy, cold place. It's something Ed can relate to. "We lived on a farm in Canada," he says. "And the pond was the biggest source of entertainment. When the air was still and the water froze fast, you'd get this clear, perfectly smooth ice. And that was the best."

But sculpting ornaments to look like ice didn't start out so smoothly. The first Frosty Friends ornament Ed made in 1982 shows the Eskimo kid scaling a big icicle. Back then, everything was sculpted from brown clay.

"It was really hard to look at that hard brown clay and visualize an icicle," Ed laughs. "It was all but impossible to work in the subtle little details to make it look like ice."

But craftsmanship means solving problems. Ed solved this one by having a plaster cast made in the rough shape he wanted. And from the plaster, he was able to sculpt the icicle's details.

After his first Frosty Friends success, Ed would go on to sculpt a lot more. He credits his active boyhood for many of the ideas that kept the series going–though he admits it's often hard to tell where good ideas come from.

"An idea can start anywhere," Ed says. "Part of it can come from walking through a hardware store. I might match that up

YACHT
CLUB

1295QX8089

1095QX5681

with an old memory from childhood. The freshest ideas seem to come from several sources, and you just put it all together."

Consider Frosty Friends 1996. Ed says he was walking near Hallmark's Crown Center Square in Kansas City, where an outdoor ice-skating rink is active in the cooler months.

"When I saw the ice rink, I must have had playing pool in the back of my mind," he recalls. "The phrase 'cool pool' just came to me, and I got the idea of penguins playing pool on a table made of ice, with icicles for pool cues."

There's no mystery where the idea came from for Ed's final Frosty Friends ornament in 2003. An avid sailor, he sculpted the friends sailing away on a block of ice–toward a bright sunrise no doubt. It was a fitting retirement farewell to the series he worked on so long.

Frosty Friends continues to sail successfully ahead, though. As long as there's fun, friendship, and winter, there should always be plenty of good ideas to keep it going. ❄

(TOP RIGHT) **FROSTY FRIENDS 17, 1996**
(BOTTOM RIGHT) **FROSTY FRIENDS 3, 1982**

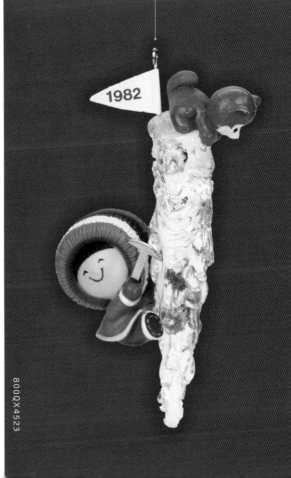

800QX4523

Best Pals

It's easy to guess that the artist who created the popular Best Pals ornament from 1999 loves animals. But look closely, and you'll notice that Nina Aubé has a special fondness for birds.

In Best Pals, Santa gives special attention to a smart-looking cockatiel that bears an unmistakable resemblance to Nina's "best pal" of many years, Opie.

Opie, it turns out, is a brainy bird who talks, barks, clucks like a chicken, and can whistle TV show theme songs—"Leave it to Beaver" and "The Andy Griffith Show," among others. "I also taught him to whistle some Mozart just to class up his repertoire a bit," Nina jokes.

Of all the ornaments she's created in her years at Keepsake, Best Pals is still Nina's personal favorite. "The ornament features many of my own pets that I've known and loved over the years," she says. "I wanted to communicate the joy of pet ownership and to capture the delight on Santa's face as he's entertained by his animal friends—just like Opie entertains me."

According to Nina, Best Pals is evidence of something that's common among Keepsake artists. Ornament designs that come from heartfelt personal experiences are often those that resonate the most with consumers.

"I'm always being told by collectors that Best Pals is their favorite ornament, too," Nina says. "This is the ornament I've received the most fan mail for. I'm always being asked to autograph it, and kids especially respond to it. I don't know how many times I've heard someone say, 'The bird looks just like my cockatiel.'"

Nina says Opie is 16 now and still going strong. He's also passing his talents on to another of Nina's pet birds. "So now I get to hear everything in stereo," she laughs. ❋

18950X6879

(ABOVE) **BEST PALS, 1999**

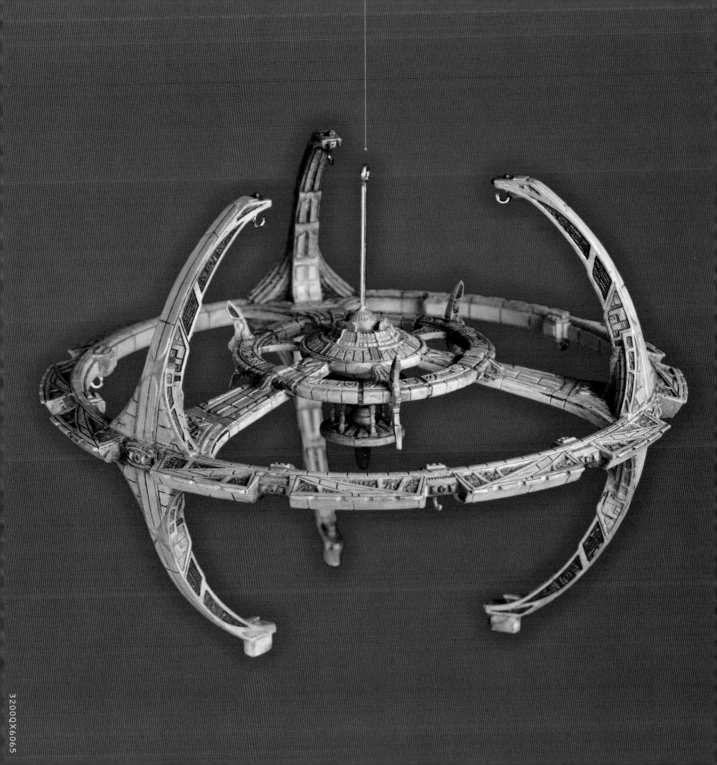

3200QX6065

Starship

Who would have guessed that *Star Trek* fans would become Keepsake ornaments fans, too? Well, Lynn Norton had a pretty good idea. He's a *Star Trek* fan himself—has been since the TV series began in 1966.

But when Paramount Pictures first approached Hallmark to create an ornament of the beloved *U.S.S. Enterprise NCC-1701* to commemorate the series' 25th anniversary, Keepsake had never made an ornament of a popular cultural icon. This led to some creative disagreements on the Keepsake team.

On one side was the "Christmas appeal" faction who wanted to have a bust of Santa popping out of the *Enterprise* bridge and a green garland around the saucer edge. Lynn and Keepsake editor Tina Hacker were horrified at that idea. Both longtime Trekkers, Lynn and Tina suspected the ornament, depicted without Christmas embellishments, could be a success, with *Star Trek* fans snatching it up alongside regular ornament collectors. "Tina and I fought for the fans," Lynn recalls. "We thought they'd want the ornament to be as authentic as possible."

Finally, a compromise was reached, and the *Enterprise* went into production with regulation Starfleet design, but festive red and green flashing lights. And it was the huge crossover success that Lynn and Tina had hoped. The 1991 edition sold out almost immediately and was put back into production the same year to meet demand.

(OPPOSITE) *SPACE STATION DEEP SPACE 9*™, 2001

2000QLX7199

"Fans didn't seem to mind the red and green lights," Lynn says. "But it was the last time anyone here talked about compromising authenticity."

The *Starship Enterprise* was Lynn's first sculpting project at Keepsake. Since then, a lot has happened. For one thing, Tina and Lynn were married. And Lynn has gone on to sculpt a wide array of *Star Trek* ornaments, including *Runabout–U.S.S. Rio Grande*™ in 1999, *Space Station Deep Space 9*™–one of the most intricate ornaments ever–in 2001, and *Delta Flyer*™ in 2002.

His sculpting methods haven't changed though. He still starts by making detailed drawings and uses engraving tools to hand carve the ornaments from blocks of synthetic wood. As a 20-year technical artist at Keepsake, he excels at the mechanical challenges of creating highly detailed models. His sculpting projects may take 80 to 100 hours, depending on design complexity. "I'm a very graphic sculptor," he says. "It would be hard for me to do characters. But we're all given the liberty here to sculpt in ways that match our strengths."

Though Lynn officially retired at the end of 2006, he hopes to stay involved sculpting *Star Trek* ornaments for Keepsake.

"It's a pleasure–and a big ego boost–to be part of such a successful line of products and to talk with people who own the ornaments," he says. "I'd like nothing better than to sculpt new starships until my fingers fall off." ✳

(ABOVE) *STARSHIP ENTERPRISE*™, 1991, HAD THE FIRST PATENTED "PIGTAIL" ATTACHMENT.
(OPPOSITE LEFT) *RUNABOUT–U.S.S. RIO GRANDE*™, 1999 (OPPOSITE RIGHT) *DELTA FLYER*™, 2002

24000QX17593

24000QLX7663

Magic

Ken Crow Brings Plastic Ornaments to Life

Artist Ken Crow had an idea for an amusement park ornament and told it to Hallmark Senior Vice President Paul Barker. As Ken recalls it, "Paul told me that if you have an idea you believe in, then it's your responsibility to be its champion and to pursue it."

It turned out that Ken's pursuit of Polar Coaster (2003) would lead him and his son, Jason, to a day at "Worlds of Fun," a large Kansas City amusement park. There they rode the roller coasters.

"As a father-and-son day, it doesn't get any better than that," Ken says, smiling. But it was job-related research, too. While Ken took photographs and he and Jason rode the rides, a small sound crew recorded the screams and racket of a real roller coaster for the ornament's sound chip. Besides sound and a moving roller coaster, Ken's finished ornament also features a turning carousel and Ferris wheel.

That's the basic story behind Polar Coaster, one of Keepsake's Magic ornaments. But the rest of the story lies in the mind of Ken Crow, where an artist and a toy maker exist side by side.

(ABOVE) **CITY SIDEWALKS, 2005** (OPPOSITE) **POLAR COASTER, 2003**

Polar Coaster

4200QLX7459

As Keepsake Editorial Director Tim Staley puts it, "I think Ken really believes he's Geppetto"–the wood carver who created Pinocchio. "And that's reflected in his ornaments. They make you feel like you're in this magical place where everything comes alive."

In 2006, Ken's creativity was rewarded with one of the most coveted prizes a Hallmark artist can receive–the Barbara Marshall Award. The award recognizes "originality, dedication to creative pursuits, and a capacity for self-direction." With it comes a paid six-month sabbatical during which recipients pursue their crafts.

Ken spent most of his six months buried in his basement workshop. He went to England for further inspiration in that country's toy museums. And he returned to Hallmark with McClinkencog's Toyshoppe–16 mechanical toys of inspired whimsy, character, and mind-boggling fun. With names like Otis J. Snozzelblast's One-Man Band and Major Sputzenpops' Fabulous Flying Machine, Ken's amazing contraptions went on display to rave reviews at Hallmark's corporate headquarters.

Though they'll never be Keepsake Ornaments–they're too big for one thing–the experience Ken gained making his mechanical toys will show up in future Magic ornaments.

"So many skills are needed for these toys–computer skills, mechanical skills, electronic skills," he says. "And the skill of working with other people–I'm especially glad I developed that one."

Though Ken is quick to point out his reliance on colleagues, his inventions all take shape in his own fertile imagination. For a kid who wanted to be either an editorial cartoonist or a Disney animator, Ken says he grew up and "got the best job of all."

"My goal at Keepsake is to make something more valuable than the plastic and electronics that it's made of," he says. "The payoff is that my family and neighbors like the things I make. When I finish one, I can't wait to make another."

And who can blame him–especially when a day's work means going to an amusement park. ❀

4200QLX7686

1495QX2135

Beauty of Birds

Inspired by Nature's Charm and Elegance

Designer Edythe Kegrize loves birds, so it's only natural she'd bring this passion to the Keepsake Ornament series, The Beauty of Birds.

The series began in 2005 with the handsome Northern Cardinal ornament and followed up in 2006 with Black-Capped Chickadee. In both ornaments, Edythe goes beyond a naturalistic rendering to stylize the birds' most dramatic and elegant features.

"I fancied them up," she explains. She notes that her birds are decorated with gemstones and design stylings inspired by the cloisonné enameling technique. Each bird bears a small holiday gift of nature. The cardinal holds a sprig of mistletoe, while the chickadee carries holly.

Before joining Keepsake in 2003, Edythe was a Hallmark illustrator known for her decorative mastery. If someone needed a design with elegant sophistication and beauty, Edythe often got drafted. She brings to the Keepsake studio a fascination for surface design and an encyclopedic knowledge of handcrafts.

As a Keepsake designer, she thoroughly researches and illustrates her ornaments in two dimensions, leaving the actual sculpting to others. The first two ornaments in The Beauty of Birds were sculpted by LaDene Votruba, who has since retired.

Edythe says she plans to choose birds with dramatic markings and plumage for the series as well as widely recognizable birds with large North American ranges.

Though every bird has its charms, Edythe is especially fond of her chickadee ornament— a subtly ornate little bird perched on a small holly branch. "He's a very stylish and dapper little fella, with his black cap and throat and white cheeks," she says. "It's just the kind of ornament I'd hang on my Christmas tree."

With The Beauty of Birds, Edythe can now celebrate her feathered friends both indoors and out. ❋

15000QX2506

(OPPOSITE) THE BEAUTY OF BIRDS 1: NORTHERN CARDINAL, 2005
(ABOVE) THE BEAUTY OF BIRDS 2: BLACK-CAPPED CHICKADEE, 2006

Angels

Blame the high cost of fuel, but the number of Keepsake's porcelain ornaments has dropped steadily over the years. And that saddens Julie Forsyth.

She points to her unofficial "angel" series, which began with Angel in Disguise (2002) as an example of the "light and airy" quality and jewel-tone coloring of porcelain ornaments.

The angel series was inspired by a Keepsake design project sketch by Joanne Eschrich and lasted only four years. But in that short time, Julie made the idea her own with the simple, elegant styling she can achieve in a difficult medium.

Julie got her training in porcelain figurines as an artist for Hallmark's Little Gallery gift line. In 1981, she traveled to Spain and Portugal, where porcelain manufacturing is an old and honored art form. There she studied porcelain mold making and learned that porcelain is not only very fragile, but doesn't permit the fine detail of resin or plastic ornaments. Fortunately, that played into her strengths—creating gracefully flowing figures in a softer, more sophisticated color palette.

Her angel series, she says, allowed her "to go back and rethink some of the things I did for Little Gallery."

The first ornament, Angel in Disguise, was offered as a way to honor anyone in a caregiver position. The other angel ornaments over the four years kept the theme of "angels among us" bringing kindness and love to children.

Julie's favorite ornament in the group is An Angel's Touch (2004). Because her daughter Brenna is a dancer, Julie says she tried to capture the graceful movement of a child dancing in the supportive hands of an adult.

"I like doing things that appear to be stopped in time," she says. "The ornament doesn't move, so I try to give it the appearance of motion."

Though she says the ornaments sold well, they were discontinued after 2005 because of their cost. Porcelain is fired at high temperatures, which takes a lot of fuel. "It just makes me sad that porcelain manufacturing has gotten so expensive," she laments. "We do fewer and fewer every year, and porcelain is such beautiful stuff. There's nothing else like it." ✸

(OPPOSITE LEFT) **AN ANGEL'S TOUCH, 2004** (OPPOSITE RIGHT) **ANGEL IN DISGUISE, 2002**

12950XG5634

9950X8983

Letters to Santa

Creative Effort as a Family Affair

Letters to Santa just might be the best example of a Keepsake ornament that became a Hallmark family project.

The ornament, part of the Waiting for Santa design collection for 2006, was sculpted by artist Tracy Larsen. It shows an amused Santa reading eight comically earnest letters from hopeful children. The coolest feature is that when you pull the bell below the ornament, you hear actual kids' voices reading the letters while toys around Santa's desk spring to life.

One of the voices heard is that of Tracy's daughter Sophie. Children and young relatives of other Hallmarkers provide all the other voices, too. "Every one of the kids you hear has a Hallmark connection," Tracy says.

Moms, dads, and grandmas who work at Hallmark brought in their budding little stars to Hallmark's state-of-the-art recording studio. What's more, the letters themselves were written by the brother and sister team of Dan Taylor and Dee Ann Stewart—two of the most hysterically gifted humor writers at Hallmark's own Shoebox Cards.

Tracy's daughter Sophie was only five during her recording session, and you can see Dad's pride when he talks about how she read her letter:

Dear Santa,

I would like a ride in your sleigh. Just whenever you can. I know this is a busy time. Call my mom—we'll set it up.

Merry Christmas!

Sophie.

"My wife Tammy coached her through the session," Tracy recalls. "She's really a quiet little girl, but she did just fine. I like that you can hear a kind of nervous little giggle in her voice."

Sophie not only contributed her voice to the ornament, but the doll on the back of the rocking horse is a caricature of her, too. Sophie also has her name spelled out in the blocks in front of Santa's desk. It's Dad's way of thanking her for helping bring his vision to life. Keepsake artists often leave secret messages like this on their ornaments—it's one of the benefits of the job. Tracy would have thanked everyone who helped out on his Letters to Santa ornament, but he would have needed a lot more blocks. ✳

(OPPOSITE) **LETTERS TO SANTA, 2006**

1000QX2563

Fairy Messengers

From Rough Sketches to Dancing in Air

K ristina Kline got her start at Keepsake Ornaments in 1995 while she was a summer intern from the Kansas City Art Institute. After sculpting that summer, she went back to school and converted most of her two-dimensional artwork into sculptures. She'd caught the 3-D bug.

Kristina's Fairy Messengers series, introduced in 2005, was inspired by the work of another summer intern. Lizette Vega submitted rough drawings for a proposed ornament series while in the internship program in 2003. Kristina saw promise in the young student's sketches, though they weren't approved at that time.

That's one thing you notice among Keepsake artists—a spirit of generosity and encouragement for one another's work. There may be lots of healthy competition for the limited number of ornaments produced each year, but collaboration and creative support is something Keepsake artists learn early—because they never know when a great idea may come their way from a colleague's fertile mind.

Kristina says working from Lizette's sketches was completely in keeping with her normal work process. "I don't do detailed drawings," she says. "All my sculpting is from pretty rough sketches."

In studying Lizette's drawings, Kristina knew she wanted to introduce her fairy series with a strong Christmas theme. So she took one of Lizette's rose fairy sketches and reworked it, resulting in Poinsettia Fairy for 2005. She followed up in 2006 with Pansy Fairy.

Kristina also made her fairies' wings smaller and simpler than Lizette had envisioned, because she thought the larger wings were a bit distracting.

(OPPOSITE) **FAIRY MESSENGERS 2: PANSY FAIRY, 2006**

"I wanted the emphasis to be more on the fairy's attitude," she says. "I tried to convey through pose and gesture what they're feeling. You can see they're not all innocent. They've got a little spunk to them."

Kristina says she wants her fairies to look as though they're dancing in midair. Their poses and expressions are inspired by the Victorian-era practice of giving abstract or emotional meanings to certain flowers. Pansy Fairy, she explains, has an obvious "thinking-of-you" expression–because pansies stand for thoughts.

Of course, lots of flowers have coded meanings, so this new series–which was planned through 2008–could go on for years. Whether it continues depends on its popularity and marketing decisions that are out of Kristina's hands.

But she knows one thing–Fairy Messengers was a good idea, even if it was a bit "sketchy" at first. ✺

(ABOVE) LIZETTE VEGA'S SKETCH THAT INSPIRED THE POINSETTIA FAIRY
(OPPOSITE) FAIRY MESSENGERS 1: POINSETTIA FAIRY, 2005

995QX2145

A Baseball Hero

Fate Interrupts a Trip to the Ballpark

1495QX15242

Artist Dill Rhodus was in "hog heaven" on that beautiful New York City morning. In two hours he'd be at Yankee Stadium to meet one of his heroes–Yankee shortstop Derek Jeter.

Dill had come to the city with a Keepsake Ornament sculpture of Jeter. He needed the All-Star slugger and Gold Glove winner's approval before it could go into full production.

Dill had been sculpting sports figures since 1995, and getting the required licensing approvals was among the many challenges of his job. His Jeter sculpture had already been blessed by Major League Baseball. The New York Yankees organization had signed off on it as well–and the Yankees are very picky about the way their classic uniforms are depicted. Recreating, in miniature, the Yankee's thin pinstripe pattern was especially difficult, Dill says.

But Jeter's okay was the most crucial. To make athletes happy, Dill's sculptures have to reflect the thrilling action of professional sports. Even more important, he has to capture an athlete's likeness and expression.

"To create a recognizable face in three dimensions, I have to research it from all different angles and directions," Dill explains. "And Derek Jeter was especially challenging. He's handsome, but he has a very unusual face."

(ABOVE) **AT THE BALLPARK 7: DEREK JETER, 2002**

Dill based his sculpture of Jeter's face on more than ten different photographs. He relied on about five photos to render the pose for Jeter's body—depicting him in a typical infielder's position of running down a fly ball.

When he'd first arrived in New York City, Dill had met Jeter's agent, who'd liked the ornament. Just in case Jeter didn't agree, Dill had brought all his wax-sculpting tools along. But as Dill was settling into his hotel room in midtown Manhattan the night before his appointment with Jeter, the agent phoned to say he'd been able to show the ornament to Jeter. Bottom line—the star loved it and had given it his blessing.

So now, with the pressure off, all Dill had to do was meet Jeter at 11 a.m. and watch a baseball game as his guest. For a self-described sports nut, "It was a dream come true." He had a quick breakfast that morning and was going back to his hotel to get ready for his meeting when he looked down Madison Avenue toward the south end of Manhattan and saw a huge plume of smoke. It was just after 9 a.m.

"I'm a real country boy," Dill says. "My first thought was, 'Man, they sure have a lot of air pollution here.' Then I saw a flash. That turned out to be the second plane hitting the south tower."

At that moment—on Sept. 11, 2001—the lighthearted business of baseball and Christmas ornaments became insignificant. There'd be no relaxed afternoon at the ballpark, no meeting with Jeter.

Though he was just a few miles from Ground Zero—the scene of unbelievable tragedy and destruction—Dill was able to get only hearsay information about the attacks on the World Trade Center and the Pentagon in those early minutes. He went back to his hotel room and phoned his wife, Patricia Andrews, who was then also a Keepsake artist. He was glad he did. "Everyone back at Hallmark was going nuts with worry," he says.

Later that morning, he went to Jeter's agency to pick up his ornament and the licensing approval. It would be three days before Dill and two other Hallmarkers, in town on other business, were able to rent a car. They drove straight through from New York City to Kansas City.

Though Dill officially retired in 2004, he still works as a freelance sculptor for Keepsake Ornaments. He can look back on a sculpting career that began in 1987 and includes many popular ornaments and achievements. He even went back to New York City a year after the terrorist attacks for approval on a sculpture of Jason Giambi (2002), another Yankee star.

But when asked what his most memorable ornament is, Dill has only to relive that traumatic September morning, and the answer—Derek Jeter (2002)—is obvious. ❈

Kris's Penguins

A Playful Spirit Animates These Polar Pals

"**U**nofficial series" is a phrase you hear often among artists in the Keepsake Ornaments Studio. It usually refers to ornaments with a certain theme, style, or characters that are repeated from year to year. They're not marketed as part of a series and continue only as long as people purchase them and the artist can find inspiration to come up with good ones.

For Kristina Kline, the inspiration for her unofficial penguin series is as abundant as her childhood memories of snowy Iowa winters.

In 2001, Kristina made an ornament of three penguin pals tobogganing. In the following years, she made other penguin ornaments and created distinct personalities for the

1500QXG2803

(ABOVE) **ANYTHING FOR A FRIEND, 2004** (OPPOSITE) **SNOW FORT FUN, 2006**

15000XG2803

young penguin playmates. There's the ringleader, the one with her eyes closed, blissed out on the fun, and the plus-size guy. Other characters show up, too, like an adorable seal and a baby polar bear. Kristina says the simplified design style of the ornaments lets her emphasize frolic and fun.

She says she knew she was on to something "when people started calling them Kris's Penguins." An unofficial series had been born.

Beginning with a light clip in 2002's Topping the Tree, Kristina started adding "simple magic" to each penguin ornament. The penguins in Pals at the Pole (2003) twirl on the ice. In Anything for a Friend (2004), the cute penguin who's loaned her hat and scarf to a snowman shivers when the ornament is wound up.

Penguins are hot now, commercially speaking–but they always have been popular. Kristina thinks we humans see ourselves in the playful penguin nature. Having grown up on the edge of Osceola, Iowa, she certainly relates to Snow Fort Fun (2006), on which you can pull a knob to see a snowball fight in action.

"I remember we had one of those red plastic snowblock makers that you pack full of snow," she smiles. "We'd make big snow forts and have wild snowball fights, just like my little penguins."

As a series, "Kris's Penguins" may be unofficial–meaning it could end at any time–but there's really no end to the playful spirit that inspires it. ❄

(ABOVE) **PALS AT THE POLE, 2003**

Santa's Polar Friend

Finding a Familiar Icon in a Natural Setting

R obert Chad has created over 25 Santa Claus ornaments in his 20 years as a Keepsake Ornaments artist. He's shown Santa as a traditional old-world figure. He's given us the American Santa. He's depicted him in humorous and whimsical stylings and even as a cartoon character.

But Robert's favorite Santa ornament shows him as a character of his wild north-country home. Santa's Polar Friend (1997) depicts Santa sharing a fond moment with a pet polar bear. There's an almost mystical natural bond between the bear and the jolly old elf.

In this ornament, Santa's short coat is dark red, rather than the bright red most Americans expect. The fine details on his clothing are inspired by traditional Nordic needlework.

The finished ornament is made of resin rather than plastic, Robert explains. That means it had to be painted freehand, allowing for his design work to come out in "nice, crisp detail."

Santa is also wearing tan boots, rather than black. And he's carrying a simple little bag at his side, perhaps filled with polar bear treats.

"I think of him as my Nature Santa," Robert says. "I think that's why he's my favorite. I like to think of him living a simple, old-fashioned life in the wilderness. He's connected less to modern consumerism than to a spirit of simple generosity." ❇

1695QX6755

53

(ABOVE) **SANTA'S POLAR FRIEND, 1997**

GIFTQXC2002

Chair and Children

Finding Inspiration From the Kids in Her Life

Every ornament tells a story, but an artist's favorite ornaments over the years often have meanings taken from her own life. So it is with Chair and Children from the 2002 Keepsake Ornament Club exclusive four-piece set, Santa's Big Night.

This ornament presents an endearing scene of a brother and sister snuggled in a big easy chair, hoping to surprise Santa Claus. They've both fallen asleep on watch, however, and missed the magical visit.

For Julie Forsyth, who sculpted it, everything about the ornament has something from her family. "The chair is just like the one my grandfather had," she says. "I grew up with that chair."

And the kids are modeled on her children, Devin and Brenna. At the time she sculpted the ornament, her children were older than the ones portrayed in Chair and Children. That meant digging through old photographs to find pictures of them when they were little.

Julie even gave the kids in the ornament accessories that are symbolic of their real-life personalities. Brenna, now an accomplished dancer, was "a typical little girl who's into theatrical dress-up." So in the ornament, she's wearing a garland from the tree around her neck. Even the doll she's holding is an exact replica of Amanda, the doll her mom made for her from scraps of clothing and an old party dress.

And Devin, who's two years older than his sister, is holding something that still makes Julie smile. "Devin is one of those brainiacs who has to prove or disprove everything," Julie says. "So in the ornament, he has a camera. He thinks he's going to catch Santa in the act." ❋

(OPPOSITE) FROM SANTA'S BIG NIGHT FOUR-PIECE SET, 2002

1850QX2566

1895QX8471

1895QX2155

Father Christmas

Old-World Figure Brings Joyful Messages

While Christians agree that the purpose of Christmas is celebrating the birth of Jesus, the holiday's secular traditions are recognized in a variety of ways around the world. In many countries, St. Nicholas, Kris Kringle, or Father Christmas–not Santa Claus–represents the season's spirit of goodwill.

Keepsake artist Joanne Eschrich's parents were born in the Azorean Islands of Portugal. As Joanne grew up, expensive gifts weren't the focus of her family's holiday.

"Christmas was all about the nativity for us," she says. "And beyond that, it was about the meaning of generosity and peace. We were told about St. Nicholas, who lived a long time ago and helped poor children."

When asked to design an ornament series to honor that uplifting spirit of Christmas, Joanne turned to old-world traditions to create Father Christmas, a series introduced in 2004 with an ornament entitled Peace.

Each ornament in the series brings an inspiring message written on a scroll that Father Christmas carries in a bag, along with symbols reflecting the message. In selling her idea for the series to Keepsake management, Joanne researched and drew concepts for ten ornaments, each with its own message, icons, and color scheme. The Father Christmas of Peace is adorned in white with a dove, a heart, and a staff topped with a laurel wreath. For Harmony (2005), Father Christmas carries musical instruments, and in Wonder (2006) he holds gifts and a snowflake staff and wears a blue coat decorated with stars.

Joanne sculpts her characters individually in wax, giving each a unique sense of vitality and appearance of movement. All prototypes were painted and assembled by hand.

And here's another family connection for Joanne–the bags holding Father Christmas's messages were all created by her mother, Leona. A professional seamstress, Joanne's mother not only sews the bags for each ornament prototype but also helps Joanne design the rich fabric coats that each Father Christmas wears. Joanne is clearly grateful for her mother's help. "I still run my ideas by my mom," she smiles. "Of course, I have to work around her busy schedule."

In terms of popularity, Joanne says Father Christmas has been the high point of her Keepsake career, which began in 1996. "I've signed more of these ornaments than anything else I've done so far," she says.

For that she can give partial credit to her family heritage. But the attraction of such enduring ideals as Peace, Harmony, and Wonder also help make Father Christmas a welcome holiday messenger. ❄

(OPPOSITE, LEFT TO RIGHT) FATHER CHRISTMAS 3: WONDER, 2006; FATHER CHRISTMAS 1: PEACE, 2004; FATHER CHRISTMAS 2: HARMONY, 2005

The Beatles

Anita Rogers Recreates a Rock 'n' Roll Milestone

W hen artist Anita Marra Rogers was asked to create an ornament celebrating rock 'n' roll's biggest TV moment, she knew the burden of baby-boomer history was on her shoulders.

The moment in question came on February 9, 1964. The Beatles took the stage of "The Ed Sullivan Show" and started into their first song, "All My Loving," while an estimated 73 million Americans watched the beginning of the British musical invasion.

The mayhem that ensued after the mop heads from Liverpool first played on America's most popular variety show is hard to imagine for those who didn't witness it. Thousands of teenagers screaming and swooning in the streets. Adults shaking their heads in shocked disapproval. And a new youth culture being born.

When Keepsake decided to celebrate the 30th anniversary of that Sunday night TV performance with The Beatles Gift Set in 1994, Anita knew she'd better get all the details right–or she'd never hear the end of it from disappointed fans.

It helped that Anita had caught the Fab Four's act herself that night. "I remember lying on the living-room rug and watching The Beatles," she says. "I was little, but I definitely remember all the commotion."

To accurately capture the birth of Beatlemania, Anita thoroughly researched the event–right down to how John, Paul, and George held their guitars and how Ringo was positioned at his elevated drum set. The sculpting took nearly a month.

This ornament set marked one of the first times Keepsake had attempted likenesses of real people. Though it's commonplace now, back then it was considered a bit risky. So Anita knew all the effort at accuracy was worth it.

She especially wanted to get Paul just right. After all, she laughs, "I had a crush on him. He's still the cute one to me." ❊

(OPPOSITE) **THE BEATLES GIFT SET, 1994**

4800QX5373

1495QX8103

1500QX2576

1695QX6349

Nostalgic Houses and Shops

Finding Inspiration From Architecture

Artist Don Palmiter has a confession. Though he loves the popular Keepsake Ornaments series Nostalgic Houses and Shops—and has been sculpting it since 1995—he really prefers houses over shops. Nothing against small business. "I just like house architecture," he says.

Conveniently, his favorite ornament in the series is a house that he's turned into a business, a bed-and-breakfast inn. It's called Victorian Inn (2002) and it was inspired by a Victorian house he saw in San Francisco. The name Karol Inn on the front of the ornament is a tribute to his wife, Karol. The two of them often stay at B & Bs on their trips.

Sometimes called "Painted Ladies," many of San Francisco's Victorian houses are painted multiple colors to draw attention to ornamental details. Don says the inspiration for Victorian Inn was a multicolored house with especially striking bay windows and a turret. He took photos to help him capture these features.

"Everything on the outside of my ornaments is inspired by actual building architecture," he explains. "I take a camera wherever I go. Then I always change things around when I start sculpting. That's partly to make a better ornament and partly because I hate to copy anything exactly."

For the interior design, however, Don relies solely on his imagination. He sculpts each tiny item and decides the color scheme. With Victorian Inn, he created two upstairs bedrooms, each with its own style of furnishings. Downstairs is the business office and parlor. And there's always a Christmas tree inside every Nostalgic Houses and Shops ornament—there has been since the series was started by artist Donna Lee in 1984.

Victorian Inn is unusual in that Don found its inspiration so far from home. Most of his ornaments are based on buildings he's found in small towns within a hundred miles or so of Hallmark's Kansas City headquarters. House on Holly Lane (1999) is from a landmark building right off the town square in Platte City, Missouri. And for Corner Bank (2006), Don turned an old hotel building in the town of Weston, Missouri, into a bank. Again, he's made some changes from the actual building. The corner entrance should be familiar to anyone who knows the main street of this local tourist destination. But the teller booth on the first floor and the bank president's office upstairs—those came straight from Don Palmiter's imagination. ❋

(TOP LEFT, CLOCKWISE) **NOSTALGIC HOUSES AND SHOPS 1: VICTORIAN INN, 2002; NOSTALGIC HOUSES AND SHOPS 23: CORNER BANK, 2006; NOSTALGIC HOUSES AND SHOPS 16: HOUSE ON HOLLY LANE, 1999**

Mischievous Kittens

Fan Stories Inspire These Playful Pussycats

Keepsake artist Nina Aubé credits cat-loving ornament collectors for keeping the Mischievous Kittens series going for so many years.

Nina first submitted the idea for the series in 1997. The name she proposed for it was Kitty Capers, and it was to be based on kitties giving in to temptation and getting into trouble. In 1999, the series was introduced with an ornament featuring a black and white "tuxedo" patterned kitten, wearing a red bow, dipping a playful paw into a goldfish bowl.

It was an instant hit.

"It's something everyone who's ever been around cats can relate to," she says with a knowing smile. She had a pet cat as a youngster, but as she grew older she developed serious allergies to them and couldn't be near them.

"People always ask me how many cats I have, and they're always surprised when I say, 'None!' I love cats, and I'm just heartbroken that I can't have them."

Fortunately, fans of the series keep her filled in on feline antics with stories and pictures they bring to Nina's ornament signings. And sometimes they have a little fun with Nina, too.

"People used to tease me that my kittens were always tormenting smaller animals," she laughs, "like the goldfish or the hamster in the ball."

In fact, the 2001 ornament, showing a tiger-striped tabby playing with a hamster ball, is still Nina's favorite in the series. But in recent years, Nina's kittens have only been up to relatively harmless mischief–like the 2002 ornament showing a calico kitty knocking over the pot of poinsettias.

"I received a birthday card with a picture of a cat in a terra-cotta pot," Nina recalls. "It made me imagine what would happen if a kitty knocked over a flowerpot–because kittens have a habit of getting into things they shouldn't." ❊

2800QX16296

Star Trek

Capturing the Personality of a Popular Sci-Fi Series

Anita Marra Rogers didn't start out as a *Star Trek* fan, but as the main sculptor of *Star Trek* character ornaments, she eventually caught the fever.

"After so much research on the characters, I couldn't help but get interested in all the journeys and battles and mysteries," Rogers admits. "And there's such depth to the characters they've developed for the various series. I call myself a fan now. Not quite a Trekker, but definitely a fan."

Her favorite *Star Trek* ornament, from 2004, is based on a classic first-season episode from *Star Trek: The Original Series*. In "City on the Edge of Forever," Captain Kirk and Mr. Spock must jump through a time portal, known as The Guardian of Forever, and come out in New York City in the 1930s. The plot, based on a story by the famous science-fiction writer Harlan Ellison, has romance, tragedy, history lessons, and a little incidental humor, of course—the winning *Star Trek* combination.

"I just love that episode," Anita says. "It has everything that's made *Star Trek* so popular for so long." Her ornament shows Kirk leaping through the time portal, with Spock close

behind, as lights flicker and The Guardian speaks three excerpts from the episode.

Getting the features just right on such well-known characters is the biggest challenge for Anita. For that, she spends hours researching photographs and clips from the series. Her goal in creating a character ornament, she says, is to capture personality—and a likeness that meets the actor's approval. All *Star Trek* ornaments also go through a rigorous approval process with Paramount Pictures, which owned the *Star Trek* franchise (the *Star Trek* franchise is now owned by CBS Studios).

"Paramount must approve the concept, the character, and the situation," Anita says. "So they sign off on everything, from the initial sketches through the final prototype."

Her past *Star Trek* creations include Dr. McCoy, Commander Data, Lieutenant Worf, and Captain Janeway. In 2006, she took on a major *Star Trek* icon in The Transporter Chamber. Press a button on that ornament and shimmering lights make it look as if Mr. Scott, Captain Kirk, and Mr. Spock are beaming off the *Enterprise* deck—to boldly go where no man has gone before. ❋

(OPPOSITE) **THE TRANSPORTER CHAMBER, 2006** (ABOVE) **CITY ON THE EDGE OF FOREVER, 2004**

Frostlight Faeries

A Labor of Love Inspires New Keepsake Legend

3500QP1662

"When starlight first twinkled on the frozen sea, a faerie was born from each tiny reflection."

So begins the legend of Frostlight Faeries, a collection which made its brilliant debut in 2001. And though these faeries do appear the stuff of magic and light on a frigid northern night, their creation really meant equal parts inspiration, planning, detailed research, and weeks of handcrafting in the Kansas City art studio of Keepsake Ornaments.

But for artist Joanne Eschrich, it was always a labor of love. And when she looks at the faeries today, she still can see the face of her young daughter who served as a model for their innocent beauty.

As with many great ideas at Keepsake Ornaments, the first imaginative glimmer of the Frostlight Faeries design collection was during an "open design project" in 1999. Keepsake open projects always mean a whirlwind of creativity in which artists turn out as many ornament ideas as they can. So the faeries began as a group of rough sketches that Joanne submitted to be put through a rigorous process of elimination, along with ideas from other artists.

(ABOVE) QUEEN AURORA TREE TOPPER, 2001 (OPPOSITE, LEFT TO RIGHT) FAERIE BRILLIANA, 2001; FAERIE DELANDRA, 2001; FAERIE CANDESSA, 2001

1495QP1672

1495QP1665

1495QP1685

1495QP1692

1495QP1695

Joanne's original idea was that her faeries would be a collection of ornaments, released in the same year, with a unifying story and theme. She also planned to use a unique approach to color.

"I wanted to do the faeries in a nontraditional palette," she says. Instead of the usual reds and greens of Christmas, she focused on cool colors so her ornaments could be displayed all year long.

In 2001, Frostlight Faeries was a sea change in the way the studio thought about design collections. According to Claire Brand, a former Keepsake marketing director, "It was one of the first times we had done a storytelling collection of ornaments in which technology was used in a big way to help deliver the emotion of the concept."

As the concept grew, the five faeries became the centerpiece of a fully coordinated fiber-optic light display that included a tree topper and a Frostlight Fir Tree trimmed with lighted icicles, flowers, beaded snowflakes, and a garland.

The Faeries were introduced with considerable hoopla. A backstory legend was created for them with both prose and verse versions penned by Hallmark writing stylist Barbara Loots. They were promoted with a four-page spread in the 2001 Dream Book and a front-page splash in the March 2001 Collector's Courier, as the Keepsake Ornament Club newsletter was then called.

The faeries themselves—because of Joanne's masterful sculpting—seemed to dance on air with an iridescent, otherworldly grace befitting their fantastic origins.

There was Queen Aurora topping the tree, along with faeries Brilliana, Candessa, Delandra, Estrella, and Fiorella. If Joanne has favorites from the 2001 collection, it would be Candessa and Delandra, modeled after her daughter Jamie, who was seven at the time.

"People would look at them and say, 'Oh my, Candessa looks just like Jamie,'" she says, still glowing with a mother's smile.

The likeness of her younger daughter Anna shows up in several of the baby faeries from Frostlight Faeries, too, which followed up the original collection in 2002.

The success of Frostlight Faeries signaled a turning point in the Keepsake Ornaments tradition. There would still be one-time ornaments and ongoing series, but this collection showed what high-concept designing, storytelling, and the latest technology could bring to holiday ornaments.

"After Frostlight Faeries came out, people at ornament signings started asking about them all the time," Joanne recalls. "I knew then that we were really on to something."

Her five little faeries had become the stuff of a new Keepsake legend. ❋

(OPPOSITE LEFT) **FAERIE FLORIELLA, 2001** (OPPOSITE RIGHT) **FAERIE ESTRELLA, 2001**

Town and Country

Hometown Roots Inspire Tin Ornament Series

The Town and Country ornament series, which ran from 1999 through 2004, proves that you can take the girl out of the hometown, but you can't take the hometown out of the girl. For artist Linda Sickman, who celebrated her 44th anniversary at Hallmark in 2007, her hometown is where memories and art come together.

Linda grew up in Clinton, Missouri. She created the ornaments in Town and Country based on landmarks in and around this small town on the edge of the Ozarks.

She says she modeled Farm House, the ornament that introduced the series, "on a wonderful old country house I always passed on my way back home. It has a porch that wraps around the house, and it was always decorated for Christmas."

(ABOVE) TOWN AND COUNTRY 3: FIRE STATION NO. 1, 2001
(OPPOSITE) TOWN AND COUNTRY 6: HOMETOWN CHURCH, 2004

1595QX8052

CHRISTMAS
SERVICES
MIDNIGHT
9:00AM 11:00AM

1695QX8201

1595QX6947

1595QX6439

1695QX8156

A barn down the road served as a model for Red Barn, which Linda sculpted as a coordinating piece for Farm House in the series' first year.

Other series ornaments were inspired by buildings that were part of the world Linda grew up in. Fire Station No. 1 (2001) "looks just like the fire station I used to know," she says. And Hometown Church (2004) was based on the church she attended with her family. "The church still looks pretty much the same," she says. "If you were in Clinton, you'd be able to recognize it."

The two-ornament set, Grandmother's House and Covered Bridge (2002), are works from Linda's imagination. But the bridge features a small-town tradition that Linda remembers well—graffiti on bridges advertising youthful romances. The names she wrote inside her bridge are those of her immediate family, however. It was her chance to give a wink to her hometown roots.

Besides the fun of recreating small parts of her hometown, Linda enjoyed the Town and Country series for another reason—all the ornaments were made of tin. And Linda loves working with tin.

In painting tin ornaments, artists have to distort their artwork to compensate for the material stretching during manufacturing. But in Linda's opinion, the advantages outweigh the challenges. "You can get so many colors and such great detail with tin," she explains. "And it's very lightweight, so you can hang these ornaments way out on the end of a branch."

The price of tin keeps going up, however, and Linda believes that's the reason the series ended after only six years. But while it lasted, she was able to share a part of her hometown with ornament buyers.

"It was fun to create something with such a personal connection for me," she says, "and to share that with people who have the same feelings for small-town country life that I do." ✳

(TOP LEFT, CLOCKWISE) TOWN AND COUNTRY COMPLEMENT: RED BARN, 1999; TOWN AND COUNTRY 1: FARM HOUSE, 1999; TOWN AND COUNTRY 4: GRANDMOTHER'S HOUSE AND COVERED BRIDGE, 2002

4200QLX7616

Rock Candy Railroad

Artist's Creations Make Showbiz Magic

Rock Candy Railroad (2006) is what's known as a "mega-honker" at Keepsake Ornaments. And the king of the mega-honker is artist Ken Crow.

"This ornament has all the lights, whistles, and bells," Ken says enthusiastically.

Enthusiasm, along with commitment to his craft and passion for animated toys, seems to be Ken's permanent attitude. He's been making "mega-honker" ornaments with lights and motion since the mid-'80s. Keepsake sound technology, which has improved tremendously in recent years, adds another important dimension to his work.

Rock Candy Railroad has music and song–all written, performed, and recorded by Hallmark writer Tracy Icenogle. As Ken was developing his vision for a miniature railroad, Tracy got to work on the music.

"The funny thing about that project was the way it grew from a simple lyric-writing assignment to one that included music writing, playing, singing, and recording," Tracy says. "It used every skill I have, plus a few I had to learn."

Collaborating with so many other creative types is an inspiration for Ken. "I compare myself to a movie director," he says. "A director relies on an awful lot of people to bring his vision to life."

In keeping with the movie-director theme, Ken says a proper mega-honker should have many of the elements of showbiz. It begins with the scene. All of Ken's big ornaments seem to take a large piece of real estate and magically compress it into a few inches. Then comes the real enchantment. "I want my ornaments to put on a little show," he says. "They have to tell a good story with action and message."

Rock Candy Railroad is interactive. You can turn the dial to send the train on a tour past Gumdrop Junction, Sleighbell Center, and Santa's Workshop while the conductor calls out the stops and the theme song plays. Just hit the sound button for various railroad sound effects.

"The key is to keep it from getting boring so someone can enjoy it time after time," Ken says. He adds with an impish smile, "Oh, and it all has to fit in your hand." ❋

Maxine

Giving a Voice to Holiday Crabbiness

Artist John Wagner says his favorite Maxine ornaments are those that let ol' sourpuss say what's on her mind. In other words, sound ornaments. And of those, his favorite so far is The Crabby Caroler from 2005.

Maxine is the crabby, blue-haired lady in bunny slippers who John started drawing for Shoebox Cards in 1986. Her fondness for "yelling it like it is" was her defining characteristic right from the start.

"I wanted to create an older woman that everyone could identify with," he says. "Someone who's been through a lot and has earned the right to say things that the rest of us keep to ourselves. Maxine is proud of the fact that she doesn't give a damn."

Maxine was inspired by John's mother, Toni, his maiden aunts, and his grandmother (who paid for his first art lessons).

"Growing up around New York City and New Jersey, I knew these women who were tougher than shoe leather," John says. "Yet they were smart and funny, and they could laugh at hard times."

According to John, 75 percent of Maxine's personality comes from the words she speaks. And with Keepsake Ornaments, sound chip technology is the best way to let her spout those irreverent quips about shopping, cooking, relatives...you name it.

"We've done ornaments without sound," John says. "But for me, Maxine ornaments really took off when we put a voice with them. The visual design grows out of the voice and verbal theme."

(ABOVE) THIS MAXINE SHOEBOX GREETING CARD WAS THE INSPIRATION FOR THE CRABBY CAROLER ORNAMENT. (OPPOSITE) THE CRABBY CAROLER, 2005

For The Crabby Caroler, the theme is the tradition of Christmas caroling–but with Maxine's own grumpy spin on the holiday classics. To develop that spin, John worked with Keepsake Editorial Director Tim Staley, who called in the humor writers to come up with the funny stuff, such as:

"I'll be home for Christmas…Hopefully, home alone!"

"Up on the housetop!...That's a good place to hide from the relatives!"

"Should old acquaintance be forgot?...Yeah, usually."

Only after he knew what Maxine was going to say did John start sketching the scene–Maxine singing with her dog Floyd beside a streetlamp. He then turned his drawings over to Keepsake sculptor Mike Dirham, who created the prototype for the battery-powered sound and light ornament.

The voice of Maxine belongs to Cathy Barnett, who's been portraying the old gal since 1998, when she was first hired to entertain at Keepsake's 25th anniversary celebration in Kansas City. Those who attended might remember Cathy's brilliant debut in full Maxine regalia...though they may not recall the guy who accompanied her.

"People would look at me like, 'Who the heck are you?'" John says with a smile. "Everyone wanted Maxine's picture, and they didn't want me in it."

But he's not bitter that Maxine gets all the attention. After all, the crabster has never looked, or sounded, so good. ❄

1995QLX7592

1695QXG5371

Noah's Ark

Humor Keeps a Really Old Boat Afloat

With only one new Noah's Ark ornament offered each year, there's always a flood of design ideas from Keepsake artists for that challenging assignment. Everyone wants to come up with a new twist on a concept that goes back to the book of Genesis. But even with this overflow of Noah wannabes, Sharon Visker's 2004 Noah's Ark made waves—literally.

But first, she had to get the idea approved, and for that she needed to do some planning. "It was a hard sell," she admits. "There's always competition, with so many people submitting ideas for just one ornament."

She started with drawings, created paper mock-ups, and worked with a technician to get the mechanical movement she wanted her ornament to have. She finally got the idea okayed when she described the unique features, including a cargo door that opens and a pair of alligators going up the ramp.

Sharon modeled her ark on a wood-carved, folk-art style with a hand crank giving it the interactive play value that always appeals to her.

"I like that it has movement without electricity or batteries," she says. "A lot of the old folk-art toys had a little string you'd pull or a knob you'd turn to make things go. That's what I was going for here. This ornament is fun and it moves."

Sharon can usually find ways to let her trademark sense of humor shine in the ornaments she sculpts. Take the whimsical array of critters aboard this ark—snakes, lions, raccoons peeking from a porthole, elephants hanging their trunks overboard, bunnies, and owls.

And with a turn of the crank, a propeller spins, monkeys scamper, a dove flies overhead, and blue theatrical waves roll by. And there's Noah, pacing the deck in his sunny yellow raincoat, scouting hopefully for dry land. ✼

(OPPOSITE) **NOAH'S ARK, 2004**

Santas
From Around the World
Design Collection Reflects Cultural Heritage

S anta's wardrobe should be as diverse as the lands where the spirit of Christmas giving is celebrated. And with the Keepsake design collection Santas From Around the World, he got a multicultural makeover.

Artist Edythe Kegrize designed the collection based on folk arts and traditions from around the world. It was introduced with eight ornaments in 2004 and single ornament additions in 2005 and 2007.

In a sense, the Santas collection got its start in 1999 when Edythe won Hallmark's prestigious Barbara Marshall Award. This honor goes to Hallmark artists and writers who have proven "originality, dedication to creative pursuits, and a capacity for self-direction." The award allowed her to spend a six-month sabbatical pursuing her art.

Edythe used that time to make three-dimensional dolls. She sculpted them in various media, including porcelain, paper, and fabric. But her main creative inspiration was in costuming them, focusing on surface treatments such as etched velvet, hand-dyed fabrics, embroidery, and beaded surfaces.

At the time she won the award, Edythe was a highly respected Hallmark greeting card illustrator. But her sabbatical work attracted the attention of Keepsake management. "My work on the dolls sealed my fate," she smiles. "It showed a certain sophisticated look that they thought would be a good addition to the Keepsake group."

Santas From Around the World was the first ornament collection she worked on. With an eye for potential sales, she began researching the project by studying a genealogical map of the United States.

"I thought, who's going to buy these ornaments, beyond Santa collectors?" she explains. "And I decided people would enjoy owning Santas that reflect their own cultural heritage."

She settled on Santas representing Russian lacquer painting, German woodcarving, Mexican tinware, Italian decorative pottery, Irish Celtic knot designs, American quilting patterns, and Norwegian intricate knits, for which she plotted the design right down to the exact number of stitches in the cloak's pattern.

(OPPOSITE TOP LEFT, CLOCKWISE) **SANTAS FROM AROUND THE WORLD: RUSSIA, 2004; IRELAND, 2004; NORWAY, 2004; USA, 2004; USA, 2004; ITALY, 2004**

1295QP1701

1295QP1714

1295QP1711

1295QP1724

1295QP1731

1295QP1734

1295QP1704

1295QP1721

1295QXG4822

Each Santa holds an object of cultural significance. The beautifully patterned robes are decorated front and back in a variety of materials–from actual knitted and quilted fabrics to porcelain and metal-plating–to emphasize the unique attraction of the different handcrafts.

"None of them represents an actual antique design," Edythe explains. "What I did instead is try to capture the essence of each culture with one of its folk-art traditions."

All told, Edythe spent several months developing the concept and designs for the Santas. Under her guidance, Sharon Visker created the costume for Mexico's Santa, while Linda Sickman created Santa's German costume. Edythe designed six costumes herself, then handed off the sculpting to others, who followed her instructions to make sure each ornament had the same basic profile and look.

"It's more about concepts and stylings for me," she says. "It takes a long time to sculpt, and if I spent my time doing that, I'd have fewer concepts and illustrations to contribute."

For 2005, Edythe illustrated a Santa based on traditional English embroidery. For that ornament, she made illustrations from six different sides so the sculptor would know exactly how it should look. It's every bit as challenging as it sounds.

"Try doing that for something that doesn't exist yet," she laughs. ✳

(ABOVE LEFT-RIGHT) **SANTAS FROM AROUND THE WORLD: GERMANY, 2004; MEXICO, 2004; ENGLAND, 2005**

The Sky's the Limit

Airplane Buff Turns Passion into Popular Series

The Sky's the Limit ornament series illustrates how Keepsake artists have to do more than simply excel at their craft. Sometimes they have to present a killer sales pitch, too.

For five years, artist Lynn Norton submitted the idea for an ornament series based on the glory days of early aviation. And each year, his proposal was shot down by the marketing staff. Finally in 1996, he brought in statistics showing that air shows around the country were drawing more attendance than Major League Baseball games. He also submitted a detailed scale model he'd carved of the Wright brothers' airplane flown at Kitty Hawk.

"Once they had that model in their hands and saw the research I'd done, they started to oooh and ahhh," Lynn says. "From then on, they were the biggest supporters."

The Flight at Kitty Hawk came out in 1997 and was an instant success. Since then, the series has soared in popularity for ornament collectors and airplane enthusiasts alike. "It turned out to be a perfect gift solution for women shopping for men," Lynn says. "And if a guy is into old planes like I am, he'll start collecting the ornaments on his own."

Lynn has always been an avid airplane enthusiast, with an artist's eye for the streamlined beauty of aircraft and a technician's love for the mechanics of flight. As a youngster, he built model planes, and today he's a member of the Experimental Aircraft Association and the Vintage Aircraft Association.

Lynn's ornaments aren't advertised as exact scale models, yet he wins accolades from aviation enthusiasts and aircraft museums for the historical accuracy of his replicas. He researches each plane extensively, and that means traveling to air shows around the country to meet owners and photograph their restored aircraft. "I become an expert on each plane before I begin to sculpt an ornament," he says.

The ornament series is still going strong after more than a decade. Although Lynn officially retired from Hallmark in 2006 after 40 years with the company, he plans to maintain his involvement with this series. After all, there are a lot of great old airplanes left to honor. ❃

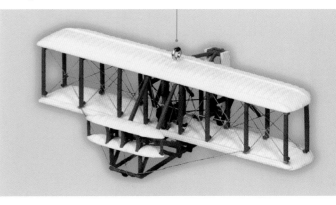

1499QX5574

(ABOVE) SKY'S THE LIMIT 1: THE FLIGHT AT KITTY HAWK, 1997

Medal for America

An Ornament's Impact Hits Home

W orld-shaking events and a moving personal encounter made Medal for America (2002) the ornament that means the most to artist Stephen Goslin.

As a production designer, Steve helps other artists master the technical challenges they encounter in creating Keepsake Ornaments. But as an artist himself, he gets the chance to create ornaments he feels strongly about. Steve says the inspiration for Medal for America came after the terrorist attacks on September 11, 2001, when he noticed that America's eagle symbol was suddenly everywhere.

"The eagle was on so many computer screens, bumper stickers, everywhere you looked," Steve recalls. "I knew I wanted to use that image to make something that reflected the outpouring of patriotism of the time."

He had a more personal motive for wanting to make the ornament, too. "I have a lot of friends who are firefighters," he says. "I definitely didn't want to capitalize on the terrorist attacks. But I wanted to make an ornament that was worthy of the sacrifices people made that day."

The ornament he created was an understated emblem featuring a bald eagle superimposed on a star, with the inscription "...and the home of the brave."

Then in 2005, the ornament's impact really hit him. Steve went to an ornament signing event in New York City. He brought his 12-year-old son Connor along, and before the signing, they visited Ground Zero, where the World Trade Center once stood.

"We were so moved by it," he says. But his emotions really caught up with him at the ornament signing later. As he tells the story:

I was signing ornaments. Like at other signings, people were crowding forward and it was chaotic. Then I looked up and there was this guy trying to keep his place in line, and he was holding a cardboard box full of ornaments. I noticed he was wearing a T-shirt with FDNY in big yellow letters, so I took a better look at him. Sure enough, he was a really tired-looking firefighter. He looked like he'd just gotten off shift. Then he held out the box and said in this real heavy New York accent, Everybody in the department's got one of these. I don't know if you'll sign 'em all.

"It was amazing," Steve continues. "Everyone there just sort of stepped back a little and got quiet. And I said, 'Of course I'll sign 'em all.' And there I am, in tears, signing all the ornaments in his box. I knew then that the ornament I'd made had gotten into the hands of the people it was intended for. I've never been so proud to have the kind of job I do." ❄

2500QLX7611

Nellco

Artist Puts a Special Brand on His Creations

The Nellco brand of appliances and electronics is really taking off. But you'll only find it where Keepsake Ornaments are sold. That's because Nellco is a fictional brand, an inside reference to the name of the artist who sculpted the ornaments on which it appears–Nello Williams.

So far, Nello has put the Nellco brand on an oven (Christmas Cookies! 2004), an antique radio (A Christmas Broadcast, 2006), and a Hoops and Yoyo laptop computer (A Christmas Greeting, 2006). Look for it on another home appliance ornament for 2007 as well.

The idea behind the Nellco label came from Keepsake Editorial Director Tim Staley. Since Nello's appliance ornaments aren't based on a specific make or brand, putting his own brand on his gadgets adds to their authenticity.

Nello puts in a lot of research and craftsmanship to keep his ornaments looking authentic, too– especially the vintage ornaments. He's especially fond of A Christmas Broadcast, an ornate radio with an elegant, handcrafted styling.

"I just love old radios and art deco stuff," he says. "They were real nice designs–functional and elegant, too."

The radio has battery-operated light and sound. The dial turns to five different "stations," with music and advertisements on each. There's even authentic old-time static in between the stations.

And the guitar playing on that rockabilly version of "Jingle Bells"? That's Nello, too. Not only has he recorded a number of musical pieces for Keepsake Ornaments over the years, but he also makes really classy electric guitars in his spare time.

So far though, he hasn't decided to give his real guitars the Nellco brand. ❋

16500XG2243

2400QLX7596

(OPPOSITE) **CHRISTMAS COOKIES!, 2004** (ABOVE LEFT) **A CHRISTMAS GREETING—HOOPS & YOYO, 2006**
(ABOVE RIGHT) **A CHRISTMAS BROADCAST, 2006**

Mary's Angels

Artist Passes the Test With Beloved Series

To get a job as a Keepsake sculptor, Robert Chad had to pass a test—turn one of Mary Hamilton's watercolor angel paintings into an ornament.

This was in 1987, and Robert was a gifted young illustrator looking for a challenge. But Mary Hamilton is a Hallmark icon whose mastery of her watercolor medium is unequaled. What would her loyal fans around the world say about having one of Mary's cherub charmers translated into a plastic ornament?

Robert took on the challenge. And in 1988, a sweet little redheaded cherub named Buttercup, sitting on a cloud, introduced Mary's Angels, one of Keepsake Ornaments best-loved series.

Not only did Robert get the job but, 20 years later, he's still sculpting the little angels. Even so, sculpting didn't come easily to him in those early days. To get Buttercup just right, he labored seven days a week, 10 hours a day, for a month.

"It was like having to learn art all over again," he says. But he worked hard at capturing the pose and mood of gentle devotion that imbues Mary's Angels. He knows how much collectors value these heavenly little messengers.

"You see the depth of meaning the angels have for people," Robert says. "Collectors always have a story about their favorite angels. They'll say, 'This one reminds me of my daughter,' or 'I got this angel right after my mother died, and it reminds me of her.' I'm always touched at how much comfort and joy they give."

He's especially pleased when Mary Hamilton herself praises his work. "One time she told me, 'I love the way you show the little feet.' It just tickled me that she would notice details like that."

Mary's fan mail includes loving praise for the angel ornaments, which are inspired by her artwork. A letter from the founder of the Angel Collectors Club of America said, "Please keep putting out the little angel beings on the clouds! I love them and look forward each season to see what's coming next!"

And in 1989, a fan wrote to Mary saying she liked the first angel ornament so much that she'd nicknamed her granddaughter Buttercup. She went on to make a request: "I also call her older sister Rosebud. Would it be possible to have one of the new ornaments called Rosebud?"

Mary, who's renowned for her kindness, made the request. And in 1990, a fond grandmother's wish was granted—the new Mary's Angels ornament was named Rosebud. ✳

(ABOVE) **MARY'S ANGELS 1: BUTTERCUP, 1988** (OPPOSITE) **MARY'S ANGELS 3: ROSEBUD, 1990**

575QX4423

Christmas Window

Real-Life Boys Inspire Artist's Creations

When you ask Keepsake artists where they get their creative ideas, they often say, "from real life." Artist Tammy Haddix is quick to add that she's inspired 24/7 by two real-life little boys—her sons, Zack and Ben.

The 2005 offering in the Christmas Windows series—a Keepsake Ornament Club members-only ornament—shows the instant bond formed between a little boy and a puppy through a pet shop window.

The boy is modeled on Ben, who was four when the heartwarming scene first wowed collectors. He's shown with his wish list in his pocket. Of course, the real-life Ben wanted a puppy, too—a connection that helped bring the art to life for Tammy.

Tammy says both her sons play a big part in her creative life and have served as inspiration and models for many of her ornaments. "They show up, either as models or in spirit," she says. "People always respond to that, and collectors especially respond to it. I don't know how they know when something is inspired from real life, but they do."

The 2007 Christmas Window ornament has two boy characters modeled on both of her sons. At first it was determined too expensive to have both boys included. But Tammy lobbied hard to keep both in and won.

"They watched me sculpting it with them both in it," she says with a smile, "so they both had to stay." ❄

(OPPOSITE) **CHRISTMAS WINDOW 3, 2005** (ABOVE) **CHRISTMAS WINDOW 3, 2005 FROM THE BACK**

Painting Barbie®

Capturing the Character of the World Renowned Fashion Doll

For Keepsake Artist Debra Murray, meeting famed fashion designer Bob Mackie at his Los Angeles studio was a highlight of 2006.

Debra specializes in painting ornaments sculpted by other artists. She was in California to get Mackie's approval of her painting of that year's *Celebration* Barbie™ prototype. Seventh in the Keepsake series, it was inspired by Mattel's highly successful 2006 Holiday™ Barbie® doll that Mackie designed.

Known for his sparkling and imaginative costume designs, Mackie gained fame working on *The Carol Burnett Show* as well as for designing Cher's wild ensembles. However, Debra says his design for *Celebration* Barbie™ 2006 is notable for its subtlety. "It has classic Hollywood glamour and elegance," she says. "It's not over the top at all."

Before joining Keepsake, Debra was a makeup artist and hairstylist. Her early career gave her an appreciation of fashion and was great training for figural ornament painting, too. "I used to make people look more beautiful," she says. "Now I make ornament characters look beautiful."

To achieve the perfect hairstyle for Barbie™, Debra adds highlights and lowlights. "Barbie™ always has good hair," she laughs. But the biggest challenge is painting the face and expression just right. "It's all those things that make the character unique," she says. "The eyeliner, the lipstick, and the correct color."

Before painting, Debra researches color and appearance from photos or 3-D figures of doll prototypes provided by Mattel. There are various facial styles used in Barbie® dolls–including a wide-eyed model and another with the eyelids slightly lowered in a more sultry expression.

Placing the eyes in the precise location on an unpainted prototype can be especially tricky. "When positioning eyes on Barbie™, one thirty-second of an inch makes a big difference," Debra says. Eyes are so important that she makes close-up digital images of them to send to the manufacturer to make sure her work is duplicated accurately.

Retired Keepsake Artist Patricia Andrews still sculpts Barbie™. In fact, it was Patricia who taught Debra how to paint the popular doll when Debra began working for Hallmark as a freelance artist in 1987. But Debra's fascination with Barbie™ goes back way before that. "I grew up in a family with three girls," she says. "We played with Barbie®…and of course we made doll clothes. I just never expected all that fun would play such a part in my future."

She certainly didn't expect she'd be visiting fashion designer Bob Mackie to talk about Barbie™ costumes someday. And what was that experience like?

"Very cool," she smiles. "He was a very nice man. And it was comforting to know that his studio is just as cluttered as my work space is." ❀

16000X2393

1295QX8314

Santa's Chair

Imagining Cozy North Pole Home Furnishings

W hen Santa Claus isn't managing his workshop or flying in his sleigh, he might be lounging in a heavy, hand-carved wooden chair, like the Santa's Chair Keepsake Ornament that artist Robert Chad created for 2000.

Robert's inspiration for Santa's Chair is Black Forest-style furniture, with its rustic, lodge-inspired look. As Robert considered how Santa might spend his rare leisure moments, he developed a deeper appreciation for the jolly old elf.

"I picture Santa as someone with a deep connection to nature," Robert says. "The natural elements have an old-world look. I think he'd like traditional furniture that reminds him of wildlife and the outdoors. And he'd want something sturdy that will last a really long time."

The chair depicts a Christmas wildlife menagerie with mountain sheep, deer, and a wreath carved into the backrest, a pair of moose as legs, and bears and elves serving as armrests. It's draped with Santa's unmistakable cold weather gear, with his big boots resting underneath.

In talking with Keepsake Ornament collectors, Robert says Santa's Chair has been one of his most well-known ornaments, and that it's equally popular with women and men. So in 2001, Robert followed Santa's Chair with a Mrs. Claus' Chair ornament. This chair still has a rugged, hand-carved look, but with more homey, feminine touches. Looking at them together, you can imagine Mr. and Mrs. Claus sitting together around the fire on a frosty North Pole night, discussing plans for the Christmas season.

In keeping with his Santa's home furnishings theme, Robert also created The Workshop Clock, a Black Forest-style cuckoo clock decorated with elf motifs, as a Keepsake Ornament Club exclusive ornament for 2006. ❄

1295QX6955

(OPPOSITE) **SANTA'S CHAIR, 2000** (ABOVE) **MRS. CLAUS' CHAIR, 2001**

Peanuts

The Wisdom and Magic of Innocence

When she was told by an assistant to Charles Schulz that the creator of the PEANUTS® comic strip didn't usually autograph his artwork, artist Katrina Bricker was momentarily intimidated.

"Then I thought, this is a once-in-a-lifetime chance, and I'm going to ask him," she says, recalling her meeting with Schulz at his Santa Rosa, California, studio. She'd made the trip with several other Hallmark artists, and the great cartoonist had given each of them a print of his artwork.

"I took it up to him, and he smiled and signed my print," Katrina remembers. "Meeting Charles Schulz was definitely the high point of my career."

Maybe that's one reason sculpting PEANUTS® Keepsake Ornaments is one of Katrina's favorite assignments. And of those, Snoopy and his doghouse are her two favorite subjects. She says it's because the little white dog isn't what you'd expect—there's a depth to him and his imaginative world.

In Merry Christmas, Snoopy! (2004), Katrina sculpted Snoopy in one of his typical positions—perched on the peaked roof of his doghouse—while receiving a present from Charlie Brown. But Katrina knows, along with other Snoopy fans, that there's a lot more to this scene than meets the eye.

"I love that the doghouse has all this stuff in it," she says, referring to reports of several large rooms inside, along with a basement, pool table, TV, and artwork collection. "And yet Snoopy spends all of his time outside on the roof. That's just one of Snoopy's many mysteries. He's a total chameleon."

The innocent wisdom of the PEANUTS® world especially appeals to Katrina now that she's a mother. "Peanuts has something you just don't see much anymore," she says. "There's such an edge to cartoons and entertainment these days. PEANUTS® can say a lot without losing its innocence."

Fortunately, Schulz was able to pass on his vision before his death in 2000. And each year, Keepsake offers new ornaments that capture the spirit of the PEANUTS® gang. Katrina has sculpted Schulz' characters since beginning her Keepsakes career in 1995. She says that getting her designs approved by the PEANUTS® licensing team has always been a smooth process.

"They're very easy to work with," she says. "But Charles Schulz had definite thoughts on what should be done with his characters. I understand that. After all, he created this wonderful world that so many people have cherished for so long."

Despite creating the most popular comic strip of all time, Charles M. Schulz did have one thing in common with Snoopy. "He wasn't what you'd expect," Katrina says. "You'd think such a famous American icon would have a huge ego, because that's what drives most people. But Charles Schulz was so down to earth and humble when I met him—just like a really nice grandpa." ❊

(OPPOSITE) **MERRY CHRISTMAS, SNOOPY!, 2004**

1495QX1408I

Queens

An Imaginative Collection Gets the Royal Treatment

If there were a prize for whimsically creative costuming, The Queen Of...design collection from 2004 should win it. Artist Sue Tague called on 40 years of Hallmark experience to create this group of nine symbolically attired doll ornaments, each one representing a different activity.

Sue originally proposed the collection as a gift-giving opportunity for women. The collection's slogan became "Ornaments that celebrate the hobbies and interests of someone you know (maybe even you)!"

To make sure her ornaments held together as a collection, she settled on a set of items each doll should have. Being queens, each needed a crown, a cape, and a scepter. And each part of the doll and its clothing had to tie in to the activity represented.

For instance, the Queen of Cuisine has a crown of silverware, a whisk for a scepter, a kitchen-towel cape, and measuring spoons on her shoes. The Queen of Do-It-Yourself has a crown of paint brushes, paint splashes for hair, and a sheet of color swatches for a cape. The Queen of Shoes has shoes for a crown, shoelaces for hair, and a shoehorn for a scepter.

Sue says that symbols have always played a part in her artwork. "I like communicating in nonverbal ways," she says. "With ornaments, you can't always use words."

Doll for doll, this collection represents a daunting combination of items, materials, and fabrics. That's where Sue's years of experience helped out.

"Each one has so many different pieces to it," she says. "I needed a good knowledge of materials and manufacturing capabilities. Then everything had to be made in miniature. It was a chore, but I really had a great time with that collection."

And the dolls surely helped a lot of women celebrate those activities that make life so interesting. So long live the queen! ❋

(OPPOSITE TOP LEFT, CLOCKWISE) QUEEN OF CUISINE, 2004; QUEEN OF THE GARDEN, 2004; QUEEN OF MULTITASKING, 2004; QUEEN OF DO-IT-YOURSELF, 2004; QUEEN OF FITNESS, 2004; QUEEN OF SHOES, 2004; QUEEN OF SHOPPING, 2004

1295QP1844

1295QP1804

1295QP1814

1295QP1824

1295QP1801

1295QP1811

1295QP1821

2800QLX7622

Rockin' With Santa

The Artist's Nostalgic Creation Is a Real Player

Millions of Baby Boomers remember "suitcase" record players, the kind kids hauled to parties and sleepovers. But no one remembers listening to the latest rock 'n' roll albums on a Viskophone.

That's because Viskophone is a name coined by artist Sharon Visker for her 2005 ornament Rockin' With Santa.

This cool little ornament comes with three mini record albums that you can put on the turntable. Flashing lights simulate the spinning turntable, while a computer chip plays three different Christmas songs, depending on what record is on.

Lending her name to her ornament is just one way Sharon brings her lively sense of humor and fun to so many of her Keepsake creations. She's especially proud of Rockin' With Santa.

"It not only has nostalgic value," she says, "but it has great play value, too. The neat thing is that it works. You can interact with it. It reminds me of all the toys and gadgets from my childhood that now are so retro cool."

Sharon got the idea for her record player ornament after researching old catalogs from the 1960s. The ornament is designed in a two-tone style with red and green Christmas colors. For the green, though, Sharon chose an aqua that looks very early '60s.

Consumers liked Rockin' With Santa, too. It was chosen by Hallmark for national promotion and was featured in a TV commercial. In the commercial, a mom is hanging the little record player on a tree as her young son looks on.

"I didn't know they were that small," the little boy says in one of those revealing generation-gap moments.

"After that commercial, the ornament blew out of the stores," Sharon recalls. She adds with a smile, "It was the number-one ornament until Barbie™ came along."

Well, that's only fitting. Back in the day, most girls like Barbie would have had a record player just like the Viskophone. ❋

Fresh Ideas

Tom Best's Illustrations Bring Ornaments to Life

Tom Best's job doesn't involve actual sculpting, but you can see his artistic contributions in many ornaments. Take Trimming the Tree (2006)–fifth in the Winter Wonderland snow globe series. Duane Unruh sculpted the ornament based on Tom's drawings of a quaint streetscape filled with holiday shoppers.

Tom also brings distinctive styles to Keepsake through the design collections he's worked on. For 2006, he created the Kid Speak group–six ornaments using innovative letterforms and collage, along with high-energy color and language, to celebrate a range of kid activities.

"Each ornament in this group was like putting a puzzle together," he says. "I was happy with how the guitar neck in Music makes part of the 'K', and I really liked the green in Video Games. In the end, the goal was to bring something unique to the line and deliver a really explosive compliment to a kid."

Tom began his sketches for Trimming the Tree after studying what had come before in the Winter Wonderland series. His inspiration was the big public Christmas trees that often adorn small town squares across the United States. For his street scene, he wanted buildings with character that didn't look too modern or upscale.

(ABOVE, OPPOSITE RIGHT) ORIGINAL DRAWINGS FOR TRIMMING THE TREE
(OPPOSITE) WINTER WONDERLAND 5: TRIMMING THE TREE, 2006

1250QX2553

12500XG3356

12500XG3346

"We live near the Brookside area of Kansas City, and that was the inspiration for my drawings," Tom says. "It's an older part of town, but it's well-preserved."

For every ornament that Tom gets credit for in a year, he may hand over a dozen different illustrations to Keepsake art directors. He's often surprised by what gets accepted.

"A lot of times I won't even know which ones are being used until I walk by somebody's booth and see it being sculpted," Tom says with his usual good-natured laugh. "But that's the cool part of my job. I can create something in the two-dimensional world and have one of my friends make it a 3-D object that I can turn around in my hand—and it still looks like my drawing. I'm still juiced about that."

Before joining Keepsake in 2003, Tom was a greeting card illustrator and designer for 20 years. He earned an illustration degree in college and has been drawing seriously since childhood. "There's always that one kid in class who could draw well," he says. "That was me. That was the one thing I could do better than everyone else."

Tom says his versatility as an illustrator has always been his major strength. "In cards, I could paint flowers one day, draw cartoons the next, and draw grandma in a family scene the day after that," he says. "Whatever you need—I'm the cleanup batter."

Because he doesn't sculpt, Tom says he brings his illustration portfolio to ornament signings to help explain his role to collectors. "It's like showing them the blueprints of something before it's built," he says. "Every ornament starts out with drawings or sketches. And that's where I live full time." ❊

Language of Flowers

These Angels Wear Messages of Emotion

1595QK1171

"Pansies always stand for thoughts...." Every Hallmark artist knows that. It's right there on the world's best-selling greeting card ever–first introduced by Hallmark back in 1939. For a nickel.

So it was only natural for Sue Tague to introduce The Language of Flowers series in 1996 with a lovely handcrafted angel named Pansy, who's holding a silver-plated container filled with her favorite flowers.

Sue has worked for Hallmark for over 40 years, both as a full-time and contract artist. In her early career, she created charming little characters known in Hallmark circles as "cutes." She says she's still known for her light, whimsical style. In that respect, The Language of Flowers was something of a novelty for her. "I think of these angels as more pretty than cute," she says.

In proposing the idea for the series, Sue was inspired by the Victorian-era tradition of giving symbolic meaning to certain flowers. She chose flowers that were popular and that had uplifting messages "so more people could relate to them," she

(ABOVE) **LANGUAGE OF FLOWERS 1: PANSY ANGEL, 1996, WAS THE FIRST IN THE LANGUAGE OF FLOWERS SERIES.**

says. "In Victorian times, when someone handed you flowers, it meant something. I've always been interested in symbols because they're another way to communicate."

Other ornaments in the series, along with their meanings, were Snowdrop Angel (1997), representing hope; Iris Angel (1998), faithfulness; and Rose Angel (1999), love and beauty.

Iris Angel also had a hidden message from Sue to her daughter Sarah. They were both members of the Kappa Kappa Gamma sorority, of which the iris, or fleur-de-lis, is the official flower because of its dignity and grace. "I wanted to give my daughter an ornament that has meaning for both of us," she

says, "and this reminds us of our college days."

Creating costumes for her angels was a creative challenge that Sue says she enjoyed. "The angels gave me an excuse to design costumes that meant something besides just being pretty. I tried to blend the shapes and colors of the flowers with Victorian-style clothing."

Though the series lasted only four years, Sue says it's still one of her favorites. "This series was different than anything we'd done at the time," she says. "It still feels real individual to me."

And it was inspired by a little flower that stands for a big part of Hallmark history. ❊

(ABOVE LEFT TO RIGHT) LANGUAGE OF FLOWERS 3: IRIS ANGEL, 1998; LANGUAGE OF FLOWERS 2: SNOWDROP ANGEL, 1997; LANGUAGE OF FLOWERS 4: ROSE ANGEL, 1999

Puppy Love

For dog lover Anita Marra Rogers, the Puppy Love ornament series was a perfect fit.

The popular series began in 1991 with a roly-poly spaniel happily scrambling up a candy cane. But Anita's personal favorite would have to be Puppy Love 1996–which shows a miniature dachshund, just like her beloved childhood friend, Peewee.

That's Peewee all right–raiding a Christmas stocking where Santa has left a puppy treat. You can tell it's him from the crooked tail that was one of the sweet pup's defining characteristics, along with his complete devotion to Anita.

"I got him when I was 11," Anita says. "He followed me everywhere and slept on my bed every night. We were inseparable."

Anita proved her loyalty to Peewee, too. Though working and self-supporting, Anita stayed in the family home so that her old friend, who was in failing health and nearly blind by then, wouldn't have to endure a move.

It's no surprise that Puppy Love was such a success. Anita is a master at creating puppies with personality–and who doesn't love puppies?

To keep interest strong, Anita modeled all the puppies in the series after the American Kennel Club's top 20 most popular breeds. But even so, she's based most of her ornaments on dogs she's known personally. The yellow lab from 2004 was modeled on her sister's dog. The adorable Yorkshire terrier in 2000 was a friend's puppy. Anita spent an afternoon photographing that Yorkie before capturing it in just the right pose.

Though Peewee never could be replaced, Anita does have a new canine best friend–not a purebred, so she won't make it as a Puppy Love model. But she's a gorgeous mutt whose photo was included in the original 2002 Special Dog photo holder that Anita sculpted.

Anita rescued her from a dog pound–so her name, of course, is Lucky. ❊

(ABOVE) **THE ORIGINAL SKETCH FOR PUPPY LOVE 14** (OPPOSITE TOP LEFT, CLOCKWISE) **PUPPY LOVE 1, 1991; PUPPY LOVE 6, 1996, IS BASED ON THE ARTIST'S DACHSHUND; PUPPY LOVE 14, 2004, IS MODELED ON THE ARTIST'S SISTER'S LABRADOR.**

775QX5379

795QX5651

895QX8441

1696DX771

Robot Parade

Imagination and Enthusiasm Bring a Series to Life

Not every ornament series lasts a decade or more. Robot Parade only had a three-year run. And when the marketing gurus at Keepsake decided to cancel it, Nello Williams' heart broke just a little.

It was one of the hard decisions that have to be made in any business. But Robot Parade was one of those intersections where an artist's lifelong fascination and job description come together. And Nello really had fun with his robots. You can see his enthusiasm in the whimsy and liveliness of his creations.

"I'm the robot guy," he explains. "These were my absolute favorite ornaments."

Nello, who started as a Keepsake sculptor in 1995, collects robot toys and has always been interested in the science fiction design styles of the 1940s and '50s– the age of Buck Rogers and Flash Gordon. He still loves the rocket ships, the futuristic cities, and, most of all, the robots.

"There's the story of my mom going to a parent-teacher conference when I was in grade school," he says with a smile. "The teacher told her I'd been causing quite a stir by going around and pretending to be a robot."

The Robot Parade series lasted from 2000 to 2002. For Nello, the time was too short, but still sweet. ✱

1495QX8133

1495QX8162

(OPPOSITE) **ROBOT PARADE 1, 2000** (ABOVE LEFT) **ROBOT PARADE 3, 2002** (ABOVE RIGHT) **ROBOT PARADE 2, 2001**

Barbie®

An Artist Spends Quality Time With an Old Friend

Barbie® doll has made a lot of friends through the years. But few know this popular fashion doll as well as Patricia Andrews does.

Since Keepsake Ornaments introduced the Holiday™ Barbie™ series in 1993, Patricia has sculpted most of the Barbie™ ornaments. Though Patricia officially retired in 2002, she has kept busy sculpting ornaments based on America's favorite doll.

It's a friendship that goes way back for Patricia. You could say her artistic research began with the hundreds of hours she spent "playing Barbie" when she was growing up. "Barbie® was more than a doll to me," Patricia remembers. "Barbie® was a real person."

It was the versatility of Barbie® that unleashed Patricia's playful creativity. Barbie® could do almost anything—be a fashion model, go to college, dress up for an elegant ball, get married. After dabbling in dozens of careers and entertaining millions of children, Barbie® celebrates 50 years of unforgettable fun and fashion in 2009 and is still a stunning beauty.

As a sculptor, Patricia has spent hours handcrafting the subtle nuances that give Barbie® such a distinct style. Every detail and pose must meet the approval of Mattel, the company that introduced Barbie® in 1959—and Patricia makes sure her work meets her own exacting standards as well.

For Holiday™ Barbie™, Mattel sends photographs of the newest version of each year's doll, and Patricia models her

1595QX16212

14750QX5725

14950QXI5049

work on those pictures. Mattel is careful about perfecting Barbie® dolls right up to the time when they meet the public. Keepsake's need to faithfully follow Mattel's vision combined with its need to meet a demanding schedule sometimes can put a sharp curve in the path of product development. "We wait as long as possible to get the most accurate prototype," Patricia explains. "As I sculpt, I'm capturing the doll at a moment in time when I know things could change."

In 1995, Patricia had just finished a prototype when she got a new set of photos from Mattel showing changes that couldn't be incorporated into her finished model. She had to start all over. "That was the year I had to sculpt Holiday Barbie twice," she laughs.

But it's the challenge of sculpting a popular fashion doll that is fun for Patricia. "I enjoy the complexity of the doll," she says. "Part of that is figuring out how we're going to create something that looks accurate but can still be manufactured. And no matter how complex it is, the trick is to make it look elegant and easy – not a mass of overdone detail."

Patricia says her most challenging Holiday™ Barbie™ ornament was issued in 1997. Mattel's photographs showed Barbie® in a white dress with ornate bands of red ribbon and lace down the front. After much thought and experimentation, Patricia solved the problem by cutting out white lace and attaching it atop the ribbon. Fabric attachments mean expensive handwork in manufacturing, but the solution pleased Mattel.

Patricia's favorite Barbie™ ornaments are those modeled on nostalgic dolls and outfits–like the Solo in the Spotlight™ ornament from 1995, based on a very popular outfit Mattel sold in 1959. "These are my favorites, because I remember playing with these outfits as a kid," Patricia says. "That was back when Mattel named their outfits and not their dolls, because the outfits were sold separately."

For ornaments like these, Patricia bases her sculpting on photographs of dolls "modeling" the outfits. The work lets her relive some of the fun she had growing up with Barbie® doll. Doing the job right also means hours of painstaking creative work. But it's all part of Patricia's commitment to the many fans and friends of Barbie®–which would include, of course, the artist. ❈

The Art of Making Magic

A successful Keepsake ornament starts with a really great idea, the kind Ken Crow gets when he imagines giving one of his Magic creations more ingenuity, action, and entertainment value than anyone has seen in an ornament before.

In the case of I'm Melting! Melting! (2004), the idea was to dramatize one of Hollywood's most famous scenes—when Dorothy in *The Wizard of Oz* accidentally splashes water on the *Wicked Witch* and melts her. Ken's idea would show the Witch actually sinking into the floor, with her black dress billowing around her and a voice chip playing those famous lines, "Ahhh!!! You cursed brat, look what you've done. I'm melting! Melting! Oh, what a world, what a world. Who would have thought a good little girl like you could destroy my beautiful wickedness? Look out, look out, I'm going...."

But between his initial inspiration and the successful ornament, there's a lot of inspired craftsmanship, collaboration, and approval-seeking. These pages will show some of the steps that Ken Crow goes through to create one of his favorite ornaments from his long Keepsake career.

1. Rough Concept Drawing

Ken translates his idea into a line drawing to show how the dramatic scene might be composed on an ornament. This drawing will have to be approved by one of the Keepsake art directors, as well as the Keepsake Approval Committee. Warner Bros. Studios, who owns *The Wizard of Oz* licensing rights, will have to okay the concept as well. After getting all these approvals, Ken shows the rough concept drawing to engineer Ron Carlson, who helps determine the various electronic and mechanical components needed to make the ornament work, as well as the external and internal dimensions necessary to fit everything in.

2. Rough Prototype

From a block of synthetic wood, Ken sculpts a rough version of the ornament's pedestal and stage where the characters will

(OPPOSITE) **PROTOTYPE FOR I'M MELTING! MELTING!, 2004**

1 2 3

stand during the crucial scene. With this prototype, he'll have to show that the ornament not only will fit into its retail packaging but that the components–circuit board, speaker, sound chip, motor, gearbox, and lights–will all fit inside. This rough prototype will be examined and okayed by the Keepsake Approval Committee before Ken proceeds further.

3. Digital Computer Art

Using a computer program, Ken creates a digital "ghosted" image of the ornament's pedestal, stage, and other technical features. This image will allow the engineer to see through the ornament and help him place the mechanical and electronic components into the design. Ken also creates an animated digital image similar to this, showing how the *Wicked Witch*

will "melt" into the floor, that he sends to Warner Bros.

4. Handcrafting in Wax

Though the ornament's pedestal and stage are designed on computer, the well-known characters will be created the old-fashioned way–through hours of detailed sculpting in wax. Ken uses an array of sculpting tools, dental tools, and tools he makes from such things as razor blades. To get each minute detail of the characters' likenesses, poses, and attire, he studies still photos from *The Wizard of Oz* and often watches the movie over and over while sculpting.

5. Finished Sculpted Prototype

With its stage and pedestal made of resin and the

4

5

6

characters made of wax, the ornament design will be fine-tuned in this step to make sure it meets the creative standards of Keepsake Ornaments and the licensor, Warner Bros. Studios. After getting Keepsake committee approval, Ken takes this prototype to the Warner Bros. Studios licensing studio in Burbank, California. He brings his sculpting equipment, too, because the licensor will have refinements that Ken must make. Among these will be changes to the number of buttons on the *Tin Man* and the length of the *Cowardly Lion's* tail. To demonstrate how she'll "melt" in the finished ornament, Ken has attached the *Wicked Witch* to a wooden dowel at the bottom of the prototype.

After receiving the required approvals, this prototype is separated into dozens of small pieces for which individual molds are made. A number of duplicate copies of a resin prototype will be created, one of which goes to Ken for painting.

6. Finished Painted Prototype

At this stage, the entire prototype is made of molded resin. Carefully following the licensor's style guide, which specifies the precise colors for *The Wizard of Oz* characters, Ken paints the finished prototype. He then sends it back to Warner Bros. for final color and sculpt approval. With all approvals secured, this painted prototype looks identical to the finished ornament, so it's used for all packaging and promotional photography. This prototype, along with an array of digital images and other support material, will be sent to manufacturing, which produces the popular ornament from 2004 called I'm Melting! Melting! ❈

Artist Profiles

Many artists have worked in Keepsake since the studio was established in the mid-1970s. The following pages contain brief, personal profiles of those whose work is featured in this book. For these and all the others who have created Keepsake ornaments, connecting with the people who purchase, collect, and display their work has always been a source of inspiration.

Patricia Andrews

Patricia Andrews was born in Tampa, Florida, and lived in England and France before finishing high school in Bermuda. She graduated from Auburn University where she studied drawing and graphic design. One of her artistic inspirations is the seventeenth-century Italian sculptor Bernini.

Patricia joined Hallmark in 1976 as an engraver and became a Keepsake sculptor in 1987. Among her favorite ornaments are her Marilyn Monroe series and the *Star Wars* series, both of which began in 1997.

Patricia's hobbies include gardening and landscaping. She officially retired from Keepsake in 2002, though she still sculpts ornaments for Keepsake on a freelance basis.

She lives with her husband, retired Keepsake sculptor Dill Rhodus, and a daughter in Platte City, Missouri.

Patricia Andrews

Nina Aubé

Nina Aubé was born and raised in the Chicago metropolitan area. She's a graduate of the Kansas City Art Institute, where she majored in design. She joined Hallmark in 1981 and became a Keepsake sculptor in 1994.

Her artistic influences were children's book illustrations, and an early goal was to illustrate children's books. Her favorite ornaments include those from the Christmas Window series (began 2003) and Ken Crow's Chicken Coop Chorus (1996), in which hers was one of the chicken voices.

Nina lives in Overland Park, Kansas, with her two pet birds.

Nina Aubé

Tom Best

Tom Best grew up in Avon Lake, Ohio. He graduated from the Columbus College of Art and Design in Columbus, Ohio, with degrees in illustration and advertising design.

Tom's passion for drawing was inspired by N. C. Wyeth illustrations and superhero comics. He began his Hallmark career as an illustrator in 1982 and joined Keepsake Ornaments in 2003.

Tom lives in Kansas City, Missouri, with his wife, daughter, and three dogs.

Tom Best

Katrina Bricker

Katrina Bricker was born and raised in Erie, Pennsylvania, where her art-teacher mother encouraged her creativity. Katrina says she knew she'd become an artist as early as kindergarten. She graduated from the Columbus College of Art and Design in Columbus, Ohio, majoring in illustration and advertising.

It was while taking a three-dimensional illustration class in college that Katrina first learned about Keepsake Ornaments. She joined Hallmark's Specialty Art Studio in 1994 and became a Keepsake sculptor one year later.

Her favorite ornaments include those based on characters from PEANUTS™ and Disney's *The Little Mermaid*.

Katrina lives with her husband and two children in Shawnee, Kansas.

Katrina Bricker

Robert Chad

Born and raised in the New York City metropolitan area, Robert Chad is a graduate of the Kansas City Art Institute, where he studied painting and print-making. His creative influences include fantasy art and surrealism. Before joining Keepsake Ornaments in 1987, he was a professional illustrator.

Robert's favorite ornaments include Santa's Polar Friend (1997), Santa's Chair (2000), and Mrs. Claus' Chair (2001).

He lives in Kansas City, Missouri, with his wife and two Chihuahuas.

Robert Chad

Ken Crow

Ken Crow grew up in Long Beach, California, and attended the University of Missouri in Columbia, where he studied art and journalism. His first professional artistic work was as an editorial cartoonist.

Ken joined Hallmark in 1979 and became a Keepsake artist in 1983. Among his favorite ornaments are I'm Melting! Melting! (2004), Polar Coaster (2003), and Circus Mountain Railroad (2002).

Ken's hobbies are woodworking and toy making. He lives with his wife and two children in Lee's Summit, Missouri.

Joanne Eschrich

Joanne Eschrich was born and raised in Fall River, Massachusetts. She received an art degree in illustration and photography from Southeastern Massachusetts University, now called the University of Massachusetts Dartmouth.

Joanne started at Hallmark in 1981 and created artwork for gift wrap and gift bags before joining Keepsake Ornaments.

She lives in Lenexa, Kansas, and has two daughters.

Julie Forsyth

Julie Forsyth was born in New York City and raised in New Jersey. She's a self-taught artist who traces her creative development back to the encouragement of parents and teachers.

Julie's sister, Sue Tague, is also a Keepsake artist. Julie has three children and lives in Overland Park, Kansas, with her husband, five cats, and a bird.

Julie Forsyth

Stephen Goslin

Steve Goslin was born and raised in Shawnee, Kansas. Both of his parents were Hallmark artists, and Steve developed his interest in art at what he calls "dinner table art school." His creative inspirations include a lifelong love of sculpture and the work of Michelangelo which he saw during a trip to Italy. Steve's hobbies include kayaking, playing bagpipes, and "bulldozing for relaxation."

His favorite ornaments include Duane Unruh's Old West series (began 1998).

Steve lives in Shawnee with his wife and two sons.

Steve Goslin

Tammy Haddix

Tammy Haddix was born and raised in Kansas City and attended the Kansas City Art Institute. She says her creative parents and grandparents encouraged her in the arts. Her early influences were the French Impressionists and the sculpture garden at Kansas City's Nelson-Atkins Museum of Art. Tammy's favorite Keepsake Ornaments include John Francis' Lighthouse Greetings Series (began 1997) and Joanne Eschrich's Snowball and Tuxedo Series (began 2001).

Tammy lives in Platte City, Missouri, with her husband, two sons, and two dogs.

Tammy L Haddix

Edythe Kegrize

Edythe Kegrize grew up in Philadelphia, Pennsylvania, where she studied illustration and graduated from Moore College of Art. She credits her grandmother's creativity for inspiring her lifelong passion for crafts and fiber arts.

Edythe became a Hallmark illustrator in 1979 and joined Keepsake Ornaments in 2003. Her hobbies include fiber arts and playing classical music and folk music from the British Isles.

Edythe lives in Kansas City, Missouri, with three cats.

Edythe H. Kegrize

Kristina Kline

Kris Kline grew up in Osceola, Iowa, and attended the Kansas City Art Institute. Her early interest in art can be traced back to encouragement from her artistic mother and a high school art teacher.

Kris worked as a summer intern at Keepsake Ornaments in 1995 while still a student at the Art Institute. She was hired by Keepsake after graduation. Her favorite ornaments include the Mischievous Kittens series (began 1999) by Nina Aubé and the Frostlight Faeries collection by Joanne Eschrich (2001).

Kris' interests include needlework, working with felt, and playing piano. She lives in Independence, Missouri, with her two cats.

Tracy Larsen

Tracy Larsen was born and raised in North Ogden, Utah, and attended Brigham Young University in Provo, Utah, where he studied illustration. He credits encouragement from his family and art teachers in high school and college for his early interest in art.

Tracy started as an illustrator in Hallmark Licensing Design in 1987 and became a Keepsake sculptor in 1995. Among his favorite ornaments are Mistletoad (1987) by Ken Crow and the First Christmas Together ornament from 1985.

Tracy's hobbies include photography, travel, and working with Boy Scouts. He and his wife have five children and live in Lee's Summit, Missouri.

Debra Murray

Debra Murray was born and raised in Clinton, Iowa. She says her early love of art began when her mother sent her to art classes as a child. Debra was a makeup artist and hairstylist before she began working as a freelance artist for Keepsake in 1987. She became a full-time Keepsake artist in 1997.

Debra's interests include painting and interior design. She has a daughter and lives in Olathe, Kansas, with two dogs.

Lynn Norton

Lynn Norton was born in St. Joseph, Missouri, and grew up in Kansas City, Kansas. His creative influences include his family's tradition of drawing, model building, and craft projects.

Lynn worked as a sign painter and silk screener before becoming a Hallmark engraver in 1966. He started working as a Keepsake technical artist in 1987. Though he retired in 2006, he is still a freelance Keepsake sculptor.

Among Lynn's favorite ornaments are the Star Trek series (began 1991) and The Sky's the Limit series (began 1997).

Lynn's hobbies include model railroading and building model cars and airplanes. He lives in Leawood, Kansas, with his wife.

Don Palmiter

Don Palmiter is a Kansas City, Kansas, native who was encouraged to apply for a job as a Hallmark artist by his high school art teacher. Don was hired by Hallmark in April of 1967 and received his high school diploma that May.

Don began drawing at an early age. His favorite subjects were cars, architecture, and landscape design. His hobbies include travel and landscape architecture.

Don's favorite ornaments include the series Classic American Cars (began 1991), Harley-Davidson® (began 1999), and Kiddie Car Classics (began 1994).

Don and his wife have one daughter and live in Gladstone, Missouri.

Dill Rhodus

Dill Rhodus was born in Kansas City, Missouri, and grew up in nearby Liberty. He attended Northwest Missouri State University in Maryville before joining the United States Army. He started as an engraver at Hallmark in 1966 and became a Keepsake sculptor in 1987.

Dill's creative inspirations are the paintings of Vincent van Gogh and the sculptures of his wife, retired Keepsake artist Patricia Andrews. His favorite ornaments are his At the Ballpark series (began 1996) and the Nostalgic Houses and Shops series (began 1984). Dill retired in 2004, though he still works as a freelance sculptor for Keepsake.

Dill's hobbies include playing golf. He lives with his wife and daughter in Platte City, Missouri.

Anita Marra Rogers

Anita Marra Rogers was born and raised in Kansas City, Missouri. She's a self-taught artist whose inspirations include Impressionist art, realistic sculpture, and a love of nature and animals.

Anita joined Keepsake Ornaments in 1987. Her favorite ornaments include the Puppy Love series (began 1991) and Holiday Tea Time (1992).

She lives in Kansas City, Missouri, with her husband, two children, and a dog.

Ed Seale

Ed Seale was born in Toronto, Canada, and grew up on a farm near there. He's a graduate of the Ringling School of Art and Design in Sarasota, Florida, where he studied commercial design and fine arts.

A lifelong craftsman, Ed worked as a carpenter, cabinetmaker, and boat builder before joining Hallmark in 1968. He was among the four artists who made up Keepsake's original art studio in the early 1970s. He retired in 2003.

Among Ed's favorite ornaments are the Tender Touches series (began 1994), North Pole Volunteers (1996), and Statue of Liberty (1996).

Ed's hobbies include hiking and photography. He has two grown children and lives with his wife in Tucson, Arizona.

Linda Sickman

Linda Sickman was born and raised in Clinton, Missouri. She's a self-taught artist who credits her years at "Hallmark U." for fine-tuning her sculpting skills. She joined Hallmark in 1963 and became a member of the first Keepsake art studio in the 1970s.

Linda's interests include gardening, woodburning and staining gourds, and oil painting. She lives in Leawood, Kansas, with her mother.

Linda Sickman

Sue Tague

Sue Tague was born and raised in the New York City metropolitan area. She received an art degree from the University of New York at Syracuse. She says one of her early inspirations was a college teacher who encouraged her to design marionettes and paper toys modeled after German paper-mechanical books.

Sue's favorite ornaments include Ken Crow's Magic ornaments. Her ornament, Elves, was included in the first Keepsake line in 1973.

Sue's sister, Julie Forsyth, is also a Keepsake artist. Sue has two children and lives in Mission Woods, Kansas, with her husband, two cats, and a dog.

SUE TAGUE

Sharon Visker

Sharon Visker was born in Sacramento, California, raised in Colorado Springs, Colorado, and graduated from high school in London, England. She studied art at Brigham Young University in Provo, Utah. Her interests include claymation and collecting vintage toys, with a current passion for mechanical toys called automata.

Her favorite ornaments include the wooden pull toys Waddles, Waggles, and Wiggles, all from 2001. She lives in Merriam, Kansas, with two sons and a bulldog.

Sharon Visker

Nello Williams

Nello Williams grew up in Safford, Arizona. He graduated from the University of Arizona with a degree in illustration. His early artistic influences were the art deco movement and science fiction art styles from the 1940s and 1950s.

Nello is a musician who plays guitar and keyboard and has performed on a number of Keepsake music ornaments. His hobbies include making guitars and other stringed instruments.

Nello says the ornament Coca-Cola®–Please Pause Here (1992) by former Keepsake artist Donna Lee caught his attention as a youngster and encouraged him to start making his own ornaments before he came to Keepsake in 1995.

Nello lives in North Kansas City, Missouri.

Nello Williams

Keepsake Ornament Club

Twenty Years of Connecting With Collectors

W hen the Keepsake Ornament Club launched nationally on June 1, 1987, local ornament clubs had already begun popping up all over the country. All on their own, folks were sharing the fun of decorating with and collecting Christmas ornaments. But something was missing.

Clara Johnson Scroggins, renowned for owning the world's largest Christmas ornament collection, remembers those early days before the national club began. Since 1973, Keepsake's many innovations had made its ornaments both highly collectible and giftable, Clara says, and buyers wanted to know more about the ornaments and the artists who made them.

"People would call me from all over the country with questions about ornaments," Clara recalls. "So I would call Hallmark to try to get answers. When Keepsake started the club, it really helped people stay better informed."

After that, Clara says, "The club grew and grew. It started having events and creating ornaments especially for club members."

Kim Jones, the KOC program manager, agrees that the KOC was formed in response to requests by collectors for a national club that could provide them with more information. Keepsake fans have always been an active and vocal bunch. These days, Kim receives a dozen or more letters each week from club members, along with hundreds of e-mails.

(OPPOSITE) AVAILABLE ONLY TO KOC MEMBERS, FESTIVE SANTA, 2007, COMMEMORATES THE CLUB'S 20TH ANNIVERSARY. EACH OF THE MINIATURES ON SANTA'S WREATH IS MODELED AFTER A FIRST-IN-SERIES ORNAMENT CREATED BY A KEEPSAKE ARTIST WITH AT LEAST 20 YEARS' TENURE.

QXC7011A

800QXC5817

GIFTQXC5609

"Most companies can only dream of having a loyal fan base like our club members," Kim says. "They're Hallmark's best customers. And believe me, we don't take them for granted."

By 2007–twenty years after the KOC began–there were about 100,000 national members, with approximately 4,000 of these being charter members. Roughly 10,000 KOC members also belong to about 400 local clubs.

Linda Nunes, president of the Michael's Merrymakers Club in Sunnyvale, California, has been a collector since 1973, when Keepsake Ornaments began. She was a youngster then, but she caught the ornament bug early.

"Christmas was always a special time, and ornaments were a big part of that," Linda remembers. "My mom would take us to the store to pick out a Keepsake ornament that we really wanted, and it would be under the tree on Christmas Day."

Linda says she and her sister, Julie Nunes, now have a combined collection of about 2,000 ornaments.

Linda has belonged to Michael's Merrymakers since 2001. The club, with its 25 members, has been involved in charitable activities since it first decorated twenty Christmas trees with Keepsake ornaments and donated them to the Sunnyvale community center, where the ornaments were given to low-income families. Club members also volunteer at their sponsoring Gold Crown store, Dora's Hallmark, where they help set up the ornament display several nights before in-store events.

Club members enjoy sharing the thrill of the hunt for rare ornaments and ornaments that complete their favorite series. They trade decorating tips and admire one another's holiday displays. But simply socializing is an important club function, too.

Judy Hull, president of the Keepsake Dreamers of Cedar Rapids, Iowa, says her club includes second- and third-generation members as well as several charter members of the national club.

The Keepsake Dreamers–sponsored by a local Hallmark Creations store–is always well-represented at artist ornament signings or events like the KOC's 20th anniversary celebration, Judy says. But club members also enjoy staging their own activities.

"Socializing is a big part of it," Judy says. "We've all become good friends. It's amazing how well everyone gets along."

Of course, other perks play a big role in attracting and keeping club members. For Keeps, the KOC newsletter, and regular, member-exclusive Web updates at Hallmark.com keep them current on Keepsake Ornament news. Members get a preview peek at each year's Dream Book, where the new ornament line is featured. They also can pick two club-exclusive ornaments for the cost of their membership fee and have access to club-exclusive ornaments at Gold Crown in-store events.

Back in 1987, The Carousel Reindeer was the first ever members-only ornament. Its availability was limited to charter

(OPPOSITE, LEFT) CAROUSEL REINDEER, 1987, WAS AVAILABLE ONLY TO KOC CHARTER MEMBERS AT THE TIME THE CLUB WAS FORMED. (OPPOSITE, RIGHT) WREATH OF MEMORIES, WAS A GIFT TO CHARTER KOC MEMBERS IN 1987.

members of the national club. The handcrafted ornament by Keepsake artist Linda Sickman showed a reindeer, wearing an ornately designed saddle, prancing inside a hoop. The design was reminiscent of the early "Nostalgia" ornaments offered in the mid-1970s.

"It was meant to symbolize the history and evolution of the Keepsake line at the time," Linda recalls.

Charter members also received the free Wreath of Memories ornament by sculptor Duane Unruh. It featured miniatures of past Keepsake Ornaments entwined in its branches.

To commemorate the KOC's 20th anniversary in 2007, a special studio piece was created, with artist Robert Chad leading the project. This ornament features miniature versions of first-in-series ornaments from sculptors who have been with Keepsake for 20 years or more. It was offered to club members who attended one of the three KOC 20th anniversary events around the country.

KOC charter member Marlene Case of Leawood, Kansas, likes the access to ornaments that only club members can buy. Marlene's passion is decorating with ornaments—and wowing family and friends with her dazzling holiday display.

Marlene admits she has about 2,000 ornaments in her collection, though she prefers to keep the number a little vague around her husband Dave.

(ABOVE) MARLENE CASE IS A CHARTER MEMBER OF THE KEEPSAKE ORNAMENT CLUB.
SHE AND HER HUSBAND DAVE HAVE NEARLY 2,000 KEEPSAKE ORNAMENTS IN THEIR COLLECTION.

"I don't like to tell Dave how many ornaments I have," she laughs. To which Dave adds, "And I don't want to know."

Dave says the ornaments that are displayed each year are rotated–"Otherwise, there'd be no room in the house for all of them."

The Cases do have a decorating system. Ornaments that go on trees are packed separately in boxes, while ornaments decorating the stairways, room dividers, and fireplace are wired to long garlands. The system helps keep their decorating time down to about eight days.

Every holiday season the Cases' home is a popular gathering place for family and friends from church, who bring their children and grandchildren. "It's especially fun to see the little kids go around looking at the sights," Marlene says.

Joyce Pratt of Lenexa, Kansas, another KOC charter member, enjoys the special treatment that members get. She says she recognized the need for a national club in the early 1980s, when Keepsake's limited ornament editions began selling out quickly.

"I could see this club coming a couple of years before it started," Joyce says. "I knew they'd eventually have to form a club and offer special ornaments to members."

In fact, Joyce has a Christmas tree that's devoted to her member-only ornament collection. But then, "All of my trees are themed," she adds–all fourteen of them. After more than 30 years of collecting ornaments, Joyce has over 4,000 ornaments with which to decorate her home. She starts taking ornaments out of their boxes as early as September, though some of her decorated trees stay up all year.

Joyce and her husband Donald belong to the local Keepsake Keepers club, sponsored by Naomi's Hallmark of Shawnee, Kansas. It's a "very active" club, Joyce says, with members volunteering at in-store events and traveling to KOC celebrations, too. Joyce gets many of her decorating ideas from the displays designed by Keepsake artists at KOC events.

You could say Joyce is well-organized when it comes to her passion for ornament collecting. She regularly checks the Keepsake Ornament Club Area Web site, prints off important ornament news, and keeps it in a special folder.

"I get everything organized so I don't miss anything," she says.

It was organized ornament collectors like Joyce who prompted the Keepsake Ornament Club to organize in the first place. KOC program manager Kim Jones says there have been changes over the years in how the club communicates with members and how it offers club-exclusive ornaments. But she notes, "The core values of the club will stay the same. We listen to our members. We're here to serve them." ✻

(OPPOSITE) KEEPSAKE ORNAMENTS DISPLAYED ON ONE OF DAVE AND MARLENE CASE'S CHRISTMAS TREES

Index of Ornaments

Angel in Disguise..40-41

An Angel's Touch..40-41

Anything for a Friend..50,52

At the Ballpark 7: Derek Jeter....................................48-49

Barbie®2: Solo in the Spotlight™...............................114-115

The Beatles Gift Set...58-59

The Beauty of Birds 1: Northern Cardinal........................38-39

The Beauty of Birds 2: Black-Capped Chickadee........................39

Best Pals...29

Betsey Clark (Musicians)...22-23

Carousel Reindeer..134-136

Celebration Barbie™..92-93

A Christmas Broadcast..9,87

Christmas Cookies!...86-87

A Christmas Greeting—Hoops & Yoyo....................................87

Christmas Window 3...90-91

Circus Mountain Railroad...37

City on the Edge of Forever...65

City Sidewalks..34

Classic American Cars 1: 1957 Corvette...........................24-25

Classic American Cars 12: 1970 Ford Mach 1 Mustang..........24-25

Classic American Cars 13: 1963 Corvette Sting Ray Coupe....24-25

The Crabby Caroler—Maxine...76-77

Delta Flyer™...32-33

Elves..22-23

Fairy Messengers 1: Poinsettia Fairy.............................45-47

Fairy Messengers 2: Pansy Fairy..................................44-46

Father Christmas 1: Peace...56-57

Father Christmas 2: Harmony......................................56-57

Father Christmas 3: Wonder.......................................56-57

Festive Santa..133

Frostlight Faeries: Faerie Brilliana..............................67, 69

Frostlight Faeries: Faerie Candessa..............................67,69

Frostlight Faeries: Faerie Delandra..............................67,69

Frostlight Faeries: Faerie Estrella..............................68-69

Frostlight Faeries: Faerie Floriella.............................68-69

Frostlight Faeries: Queen Aurora Tree Topper....................66, 69

Frosty Friends 17..28

Frosty Friends 24...27-28

Frosty Friends 3..26, 28

Gentle Blessings..18-19

Holiday Barbie® 1...114

Holiday Barbie® 5..113,115

I'm Melting! Melting!...116-119

The Language of Flowers 1: Pansy Angel...............................106

The Language of Flowers 2: Snowdrop Angel............................107

The Language of Flowers 3: Iris Angel..............................107

The Language of Flowers 4: Rose Angel...........................107

Letters to Santa..42-43

Manger Scene..22-23

Mary's Angels 1: Buttercup...88

Mary's Angels 3: Rosebud..88-89

Medal for America...84-85

Merry Christmas, Snoopy!...96-97

Mischievous Kittens 1..62-63

Mischievous Kittens 3..62-63

Mrs. Claus' Chair...95

Music...102,104

Noah's Ark..78-79

Nostalgic Houses and Shops 23: Corner Bank................60-61

Nostalgic Houses and Shops 16: House on Holly Lane.....60-61

Nostalgic Houses and Shops 1: Victorian Inn.................60-61

Pals at the Pole...52

Polar Coaster...34-35

Puppy Love 1..108-109

Puppy Love 6..108-109

Puppy Love 14..108-109

Queen of Cuisine...98-99

Queen of Do-It-Yourself..98-99

Queen of Fitness...99

Queen of Multitasking..99

Queen of Shoes...98-99

Queen of Shopping..99

Queen of the Garden...99

Robot Parade 1...110-111

Robot Parade 2...111

Robot Parade 3...111

Rock Candy Railroad..74-75

Rockin' With Santa...100-101

Rocking Horse 1..18

Runabout–U.S.S. Rio Grande™.....................................32-33

Santa With Elves..22-23

Santa's Big Night...54-55

Santa's Chair..94-95

Santa's Polar Friend..53

Santas From Around the World: England..........................82

Santas From Around the World: Germany..........................82

Santas From Around the World: Ireland.........................80-81

Santas From Around the World: Italy.............................80-81

Santas From Around the World: Mexico.............................82

Santas From Around the World: Norway.........................80-81

Santas From Around the World: Russia..........................80-81

Santas From Around the World: USA..............................80-81

Santas From Around the World: USA..............................80-81

Sky's the Limit 1: The Flight at Kitty Hawk........................83

Snow Fort Fun...51-52

Space Station Deep Space 9™......................................30, 32

St. Nick...21

Starship Enterprise™..31-32

Tin Locomotive 1...18

Town and Country 1: Farm House...............................70, 72-73

Town and Country 3: Fire Station No. 1.........................70, 73

Town and Country 4: Grandmother's House and Covered Bridge...72-73

Town and Country 6: Hometown Church........................71, 73

Town and Country Complement: Red Barn.....................72-73

The Transporter Chamber...64-65

Video Games..102, 104

Winter Wonderland 5: Trimming the Tree.....................102-103

Wreath of Memories..134, 136

Yuletide Treasures 1: Santa...4

Hallmark Is Grateful to the Following For Properties Featured in This Book:

BARBIE™
Celebration Barbie™ Ornament
Holiday™ Barbie™ Ornament
Solo in the Spotlight™ Barbie™ Ornament
BARBIE and associated trademarks and trade dress are owned by,
and used under license from Mattel, Inc. © 2007 Mattel, Inc.
All Rights Reserved.

Beatles™
BEATLES™ PRODUCT © Apple Corps LTD & TM.
Licensed by: Determined Productions, Inc.

Chevrolet® Corvette®
Chevrolet, Corvette and Emblems and Body Design are used under license.

Derek Jeter
© 2007 MLBPA. Derek Jeter used under license.

Ford Mustang
Ford Mustang used under license from Ford Motor Company.

Peanuts®
PEANUTS © United Feature Syndicate, Inc.

Star Trek™
Space Station Deep Space 9™
Starship Enterprise™
Runabout U.S.S. Rio Grande™
Delta Flyer™
The Transporter Chamber
"City on the Edge of Forever"
® & © 2007 CBS Studios Inc. All Rights Reserved.
STAR TREK and related marks are trademarks of CBS Studios Inc.

The Wizard of Oz™
THE WIZARD OF OZ and all related characters and elements
are trademarks of and © Turner Entertainment Co.
Judy Garland as Dorothy from THE WIZARD OF OZ.
(s07)

John Peterson

joined Hallmark as a full-time writer in 1992. It was his 39th job. Among the 38 previous occupations were oil rig worker, truck driver, social worker, and small-town newspaper editor. These far-ranging experiences may explain, at least in part, John's equally far-ranging diversity as a writer. His newspaper background, along with training in journalism, served him well in creating this book. It has been an investigative process, including interviews with Keepsake artists and staff, stacks of research in various media, more interviews with Keepsake collectors and Keepsake Ornament Club members, and education in technical aspects of materials, sculpting, and manufacturing. It's all added a certain expertise in Keepsake Ornaments and the people who create and own them to John's expansive body of knowledge.

John was born in Storm Lake, Iowa, and raised in Sioux City, Iowa. He graduated from the University of Iowa, where he studied journalism and English literature. In his spare time, he is likely to be bicycling, motorcycle touring, or just relaxing with his wife and five cats.

If you have enjoyed this book, we'd love to hear from you.

Please send comments to:

Book Feedback
2501 McGee
Mail Drop 215
Kansas City, MO 64108

Or e-mail us at:
booknotes@hallmark.com